PRAYING FAITH

THOMAS P. DOOLEY, PH.D.

PRAYING FAITH

*I LIVE by the FAITH
of the SON of GOD*

Destiny Image₍ᵣ₎ Publishers, Inc.
P.O. Box 310
Shippensburg, PA 17257-0310

"Speaking to the Purposes of God for This Generation
and for the Generations to Come"

ISBN 0-7684-2964-1

For Worldwide Distribution
Printed in the U.S.A.

This book and all other Destiny Image, Revival Press, MercyPlace,
Fresh Bread, Destiny Image Fiction, and Treasure House books are available
at Christian bookstores and distributors worldwide.

1 2 3 4 5 6 7 8 9 10 / 09 08 07 06 05 04

For a U.S. bookstore nearest you, call
1-800-722-6774.

For more information on foreign distributors, call
717-532-3040.

Or reach us on the Internet:
www.destinyimage.com

DEDICATION

This book is dedicated to my best friend—Laura, my precious wife with a quiet and gentle spirit, and to our four blessed children—Isaac, Catherine, Jeannette, and Thomas. Each of you is loved and favored by our all-sufficient God and by me. Please remember, *"Have I not commanded you, be **strong** and **courageous**, for the Lord your God is with you wherever you go"* (Josh. 1:9).

ENDORSEMENTS

I always look for something that comes into my path that will enhance my faith and cause me to be more passionate in prayer. When I picked up *Praying Faith* by Dr. Tom Dooley, I knew I had something that was not common. Not only is it filled with experience and research but it presents *faith* from an aspect that I have not fully seen before. To understand faith from a Kingdom standpoint, *Praying Faith* develops a presentation that is very unique. I personally have written a book on faith, but this book moves us into a new dimension of intensity.

Dr. Chuck D. Pierce
President of Glory of Zion International,
Vice President of Global Harvest Ministries, and Author

Dr. Tom Dooley is very much at home in two worlds: the Mediterranean culture of the first century A.D. and that of the twenty-first as well. Using the famous Gospel account of Jesus healing the servant of the centurion at Capernaum as his opening wedge, Dooley plumbs the depths of not just *belief*, but the kind of profound faith that can move mountains or heal people.

Dr. Paul L. Maier
Professor of History at Western Michigan University
and Award-winning Bestseller Author

It is refreshing to read a book by a high-level scientist who believes the Bible, combines the Word and the Spirit, and who practices what he preaches. Read this book carefully and be blessed.

Dr. R.T. Kendall
Former Pastor of Westminster Chapel, London, England and Author

A captivating story. This is a story of one man's walk to fulfill the leadership of the Holy Spirit in his life. I would recommend the reading of this book to everyone searching to give leadership of their lives for service in the Kingdom.

Dois I. Rosser, Jr.
Founder and Chairman of International Cooperating Ministries

Dr. Tom Dooley, a scientist-entrepreneur turned prophet-missionary, shifted his paradigm of *see before believing* to *believe before seeing* in his book *Praying Faith*. This is a joyful celebration of the mystery of man touching the Almighty to release power. I highly recommend this book for everyone wanting to increase his or her abundance in spiritual experience and life.

Rev. KC John
Chairman of Word Telecasting Company Ltd., India

The depth of insight that Dr. Tom Dooley brings to the Body of Christ is refreshing and well timed. In the coming days it will require the saints, including marketplace ministers, to have a steadfast faith, integrity, and a Rock-solid foundation to bring forth God's Kingdom for the world to see.

Bill Thomas
President of Christian Benefits Association and
Board of Christian International Business Network

Dr. Tom Dooley, in his book, provides us the theological foundations of genuine faith coupled with honestly sharing first-hand missions and business experiences and perspectives, which he gained while acting on his intense faith in God. Therefore, it is a must-read book for those who aspire to accomplish great things for a great God in this generation.

Rev. Saji Lukos
Founder of Reaching Indians Ministry International (Mission India)

Are you concerned about God's direction in your life? If so, you will greatly profit from Dr. Tom Dooley's biblical insights and from the transparent sharing of his remarkable life experiences. It will rejoice your heart to see how he is finding wisdom and direction from the Word of God as sufficient for every area of life. Tom Dooley is a scholar and scientist who has entered into a vital and contagious relationship with the Lord and Savior of mankind. The truths and insights of these pages will enrich your walk with Christ.

Pastor Richard P. Carlson
Superintendent of the Intermountain West District,
Evangelical Free Church of America

I believe that Dr. Tom Dooley has written one of the most definitive books on faith that is being published in our day. His experiences and insights have challenged me to "step up" to a higher and more sanctified walk of faith in Christ. A walk, which is, sad to say, barely recognized in the established church today. Dr. Dooley has helped to show us that faith, which pleases God, will cause us to abandon ourselves to an ongoing journey that will bring Him glory. I emphatically recommend that this book be read and shared.

Dee Baxter
President of Baxter Bible Ministries

A gold mine of inspiring truths born out of practical experience! The Body of Christ needs this book.

Pastor Chris Hodges
Church of the Highlands, Birmingham, Alabama

TABLE OF CONTENTS

Part I ✦ Understanding Faith

Part II ✦ Understanding Prayer

Part III ✦ Understanding the Kingdom

FOREWORD

Many people write forewords to books based upon the content of the book. I am writing this foreword based on the content of Tom Dooley's life and character, because he is a man who lives what he writes. As you read this book, you will meet an intensely passionate brother who is completely committed to seeing the present prophetic purposes of God accomplished, not only in his own life, but also in the lives of all those he can influence.

He understands what God is doing in the restoration of the Church to her apostolic, prophetic, and Hebraic roots. He knows the importance of Israel in the present purposes of God and of the restoration of the Church to her Romans 11 relationship with the Jewish people. He is "flowing in the river" of God's present outpouring and is seeking to walk in the fulfillment of God's personal calling to be a conduit in, and of, that river.

A highly educated scientist, Tom Dooley is also a man of deep compassion and concern for the welfare of others. He goes to places where others would rather just send money, so that he can personally impact the people who are there with the truths and realities of the Kingdom of God. Not only is he willing to travel to those kinds of places, but he is also willing to take on prayer burdens and intercessory assignments that others shun because of the intensity of the battle.

A vessel designed by the Master's hand for the battlefield, I have watched as Tom has spiritually progressed and matured. He is a man who knows how to successfully wage war against principalities and powers. He has tested his weapons and armor in the battles of life, and learned the lessons of faith he is writing about. What you read about in this book is not mere theory or academic theology, but hard-won victories bearing eternal fruit.

Unembarrassed and unstopped by what people say or think, unimpressed by academic degrees or money, he is a man who will speak and do what the Lord declares without concern for personal consequences. He is also a man with a teachable spirit who is open to correction and adjustment. His life and ministry will bless, encourage, and challenge you to grow to your next level in God.

You will meet Tom Dooley in the pages of this book, and I pray that as you do, you will also meet the Lord Jesus in a fuller way and receive a greater impartation of His faith, so that the passion of the Spirit of God deep within you will be ignited by the fresh fire of Heaven, and you experience the life-changing power of intense faith.

Dr. Howard Morgan
Howard Morgan Ministries and
Kingdom Ministries International

Part I

✦

Understanding Faith

Chapter One

THE CENTURION'S INTENSE FAITH

I tell you the truth, I have not found anyone in Israel with such **great faith** (Matthew 8:10b, emphasis added).

In the Gospel of Matthew chapter 8, Jesus encountered a delightful expression of intense faith that amazed Him.

When Jesus had entered Capernaum, a centurion came to Him, asking for help. "Lord," he said, "my servant lies at home paralyzed and in terrible suffering." Jesus said to him, "I will go and heal him." The centurion replied, "Lord, I do not deserve to have You come under my roof. But just say the word, and my servant will be healed. For I myself am a man under **authority**, *with soldiers under me. I tell this one, 'Go,' and he goes; and that one, 'Come,' and he comes. I say to my servant, 'Do this,' and he does it." When Jesus heard this, He was astonished and said to those following Him, "I tell you the truth, I have not found anyone in Israel with such* **great faith.**"*...Then Jesus said to the centurion, "Go! It will be done just as you believed it would." And his servant was healed at that very hour* (Matthew 8:5-10,13, emphasis added).

Why was it that Jesus was so astonished at the faith of this foreigner? The Roman occupiers were oppressive Gentile "lords" who suppressed the freedoms and rights of the locals in Judea. Most of them were not friends of the Jews. They were enemies, outsiders, and dogs. Most Romans were likely not well-trained in the things of God from the Hebrew Scriptures (Old Testament) and in Hebraic cultural traditions. Yet, this one Gentile centurion assigned to oversee approximately 80 soldiers, knew more about genuine faith in the God of Abraham, Isaac, and Jacob than *all* of the religious Jews of that region.

The piercing indictment *"...I have not found **anyone** in Israel with such great faith..."* included all of the Levitical Rabbinic teachers of the Torah and even all of Jesus' hand-chosen disciples. Jesus' own words declared that He hadn't seen this level of faith operating in a single Jew, including those associated with Him. Honestly, that would have stung in embarrassment. But, Jesus knew a principle of truth when He witnessed it. As He was often prone to do, Jesus used a "chance" divine encounter with a stranger to illuminate what real faith should resemble from a heavenly perspective. Shouldn't we earnestly desire the same spoken commendation of Jesus, that is, that we, too, have *great faith*?

POWER IS RELEASED WHEN AUTHORITY IS PRESENT

With this remarkable statement by Jesus in mind, what does this Scripture teach us about genuine faith that so stirred the heart of Jesus? What easily comes to mind are two things that a military commander knows well from experience—*authority* and *power*—albeit through military force. A centurion receives orders from his superiors and he gives orders to his subordinates. Successful missions are based on how closely orders are obeyed and executed by subordinates within the chain of command. Failure to follow orders can result in casualties and loss of lives and battles. Orders are meant to be taken literally and immediately by subordinates without question. This centurion knew the authority that empowers a military order.

Authority transforms mere words into actions that must occur. Unfortunately many Westerners have a cavalier attitude toward the inherent and imputed value of words. Many Westerners see them as just neutral and ineffectual terms of a lexicon. But, in the hands of one trained in the chain-of-command structure of the military, words and orders are not neutral. They carry power that results in actions. Jesus wasn't speaking with a Ph.D. university professor of rhetoric about the possible meanings of words. Jesus was standing before a military commander!

Another key to this event is that this Gentile knew who to ask. He knew that Jesus had the authority to heal on Earth, which the military leader himself lacked. The centurion didn't have supernatural power, only natural power. He had probably heard stories of the Jewish Rabbi, Jesus, healing other people in that region. The commander knew that if the one with authority simply said, "Let this happen," then the authority within his words would literally cause it to happen. This commander didn't need to see anything with his eyes of sight. He knew that the power was in the words that were declared.

Jesus was different from other "religious" men, and this Roman had placed his faith in the declared words of Jesus. The Jewish Messiah not only spoke the truth, but He spoke the truth with authority, just like a military commander with the force to see that it was done as he had commanded. One of His close disciples wrote about Jesus, "...*the crowds were amazed at His teaching, because He taught as one who had* **authority**, *and not as their teachers of the law*" (Mt. 7:28-29). Jesus was more than a teacher of the Torah, He demonstrated amazing miracle-working power through the authority within His words (see Lk. 4:32). What Jesus declared came true. He did not speak idle words. All His words carried truth and to full effect.

The power in a statement comes as a result of the authority of the one giving the message. A person possessing power can deliver a powerful message in faith. Conversely, a person lacking power, as evidenced by a lack of testimonies of authentic faith experiences, likely lacks the authority to speak in confidence about faith and related issues. They just seem to make noise with their lips, even if they are speaking from Scripture. Jesus wasn't like that. Jesus knew the power and authority that He possessed. His anointing from the Father God was in power and authority. When words came off His lips, they were fully effective regardless of whether they were sweet words of blessing to a child or harsh words of cursing in a rebuke to a prideful religious teacher. He always spoke the truth with authority in love and power. And, He still does to this very day. The Son of God "*...has **authority** on earth to forgive sins...*" (Mt. 9:6, emphasis added), and "*...all **authority** in heaven and on earth...*" (Mt. 28:18, emphasis added), and "***authority** to lay it* [His life] *down and **authority** to take it up again*" (Jn. 10:18, emphasis added). Jesus has unlimited power to do anything that He desires, from forgiving sins, to raising the dead in resurrection power, to ordering the mobilization of angels into action. Jesus has ultimate veto power over the affairs of all of mankind and the adversary, satan and all of his subordinate principalities and demonic hosts.

Jesus knew the power of authority, because He was in submission to His Father in Heaven in everything that He did. Jesus respected authority—the highest authority in the universe. Jesus did nothing without being in submission to His Father's will. To more fully appreciate that relationship between Jesus and His Father, I recommend that you study and meditate in the entire Gospel of John. When Jesus remarked favorably about the centurion's understanding of authority as the basis for effective faith, He knew well the power of following a chain-of-command structure. Jesus was acting on orders from His Father, just as an experienced soldier knows well the chain-of-command structure in a military context. We, too have a chain of command over us. We appeal through the authority inherent in Jesus' name, and the Father listens to us. We don't perform the miracles *per se*. Rather, He performs them through us as channels, as we release true words of faith.

Oh please, my brothers and sisters in Jesus! Don't you see that the power to accomplish a miracle is in Jesus' spoken words? Don't you see that the power to accomplish a miracle is in our Holy Spirit-inspired spoken words as ambassadors of Jesus, who in turn received His earthly authority from His Father? We aren't the natural sources of the power; we're just the conduit through which it flows. May I remind you that the power that created the universe was God's spoken Word, and some of which is recorded in the Bible. Words are extremely powerful! This is why we must carefully consider our own spoken and written words (see Matt. 12:36; Jas. 3:1-12). We must respect the written Word of God.

This Gentile soldier knew from experience that his very life depended on the validity of orders that were given and were to be performed. We can easily imagine that his superiors spoke like Yul Brenner as the Egyptian pharaoh in the movie *The Ten Commandments*, declaring, "So it be written, so it be done!" What the commanding officers spoke would come to pass and he, the subordinate, would do it. If the centurion spoke the words, then his subordinates would do it, plain and simple. He could trust the authority and chain of command that it would be done. The authority of the person is imputed into the words that flow out of them. The words flowing out of God Almighty are alive (see Heb. 4:12) and have miracle-working power, blessings, and curses embedded within them. They will not return void. Isaiah wrote, *"So is My word that goes out from My mouth: It will not return to Me empty, but will accomplish what I desire and achieve the purpose for which I sent it"* (Is. 55:11). Words of genuine faith can mobilize the angels and forces of the heavenly realm to action. The tongue may be a very small device (see Jas. 3), but it can accomplish things of superlative magnitude.

So, do you as a believer in Jesus have authority to speak into being those things which are not? Do you? God grants His authority to His disciples who are obedient to Him in righteous living. Didn't Jesus deputize His own disciples and send them out two-by-two with a certain authority so that their words would affect circumstances? We, too, as modern-day disciples, can work miracles using the same power of the spoken word. But, we must recognize that it is God Almighty fulfilling the spoken word, and not us. Moreover, we must first hear from Him before taking action.

INTEGRITY EMPOWERS OUR WORDS

We have the choice to speak either with or without authority. Some words lack authority based on their source, its validity, or the person delivering the message. A message delivered by someone lacking integrity is a message lacking authority. In order for a message to carry inherent or imputed authority, it must be delivered by truthful men and women, who operate with integrity. One of the single greatest disqualifiers of a prophetic message or prophetic ministry is if the individual does not consistently dwell on the truth. Dishonesty is the major disqualifier of prophetic messages and ministries. God shall not be mocked; He will not bless those who speak or write with dishonesty. His nature is honest and true. El Shaddai detests dishonesty. Study the Book of Proverbs and it will be made clear that the Lord (Adonai) is appalled at dishonesty. Yet, our modern Western society today does not hold to a standard of honesty. Our culture actually encourages dishonesty as the new enlightened *what's-in-it-for-me* selfish standard, which is so prevalent today. Intentional or gratuitous lies are commonplace within all demographics of society, even by the so-called leaders of our nations and businesses. This is sin.

I am very grateful for an incident in my early childhood that taught me about honesty. I was about five years old on our family farm in Good Intent, an area near Atchison, Kansas. I was playing in my father's workshop when I accidentally broke a drill bit for an electric power drill. I then attempted to conceal the matter by crawling under the foundation of one of our barns to bury the evidence, thinking that no one would find out. My dad, Thomas E. Dooley, an imposing, tall, muscular farmer in bib overalls, witnessed the hilarious procession from workshop to barn. As I emerged from the tiny crawl space, he asked me what I was doing. I attempted to make up some silly, dishonest story as a cover-up for my odd behavior. But, Dad knew what I had done. He wasn't fooled. *"The eyes of the Lord are everywhere, keeping watch on the wicked and the good"* (Prov. 15:3). That day started to teach me a key lesson that developed firmly within me from early childhood—respect for the truth and contempt for lying, which is directly related to the fear of the Lord. It was a substantial deterrent in my life. Ever since then, I have striven to speak the truth. And to someone for whom the truth has become a deeply held virtue and habit, it is quite difficult for me to do otherwise.

Since all words spoken can never be taken back after the fact, we must be careful to not share false, misleading, or careless words. We will be held accountable for them in the heavenly realm. When words have left our mouths or keyboards or pens, they can't be erased from an eternal perspective. The common expression, *"Sticks and stones may break your bones, but words will never harm you"* is not true. Words are incredibly powerful in both the natural and spiritual realms. The Book of Proverbs speaks volumes to the issue of our speech. For instance, Proverbs speaks of words and gossip going down into our inner most being like delicate, tasty morsels. Just as our choices of food and drink either nourish or contaminate the body, so the "right" words produce blessings and those that are "wrong" produce curses. It is even possible to speak true words, and do so in a variety of harmful ways, such as slander, gossip, deception, or false testimony. Scriptures say many times that He detests dishonesty and false testimony. We must therefore speak the truth in love at all times.

THE CENTURION'S ARMOR AND EPHESIANS 6

I have a profound fondness of the story in Matthew 8. On a Saturday morning in September 1998, while I was holding my youngest son Thomas' hand and talking with him, I experienced a daytime trance (or vision). It was as if my son's room entirely disappeared and I was transported in time and space to witness the centurion approaching Jesus and bowing down before Him on a dusty narrow road in ancient Judea. During this amazing vision, God revealed to me that I had received the *gift of faith* (see 1 Cor. 12:9). I was shocked to witness this event, and in all honesty, was surprised to learn that I had this spiritual gift. I knew of several other spiritual gifts that I possessed at that time, but this was a revelation and/or impartation about another divine gift. *[Please note for clarity that there is a difference between "faith" in general and the "spiritual gift of faith." All believers must have faith, but the latter carries a supernatural anointing to operate within this realm with regularity and greater ease than other individuals lacking that gift.]*

Shortly after experiencing the trance-vision of Matthew 8, I felt a prompting in my spirit and purchased a replica of Roman centurion armor. I occasionally preach adorned in this armor that serves as an "altar of remembrance" of that graphic vision. Added to this story, in May 2003 in Atlanta, Georgia, I had requested prayer from a prophetic brother, Dale Karoff and his wife, while attending a Kingdom Ministries International annual conference. I don't recall having met him previously. As Dale was facing me and praying, the Holy Spirit revealed several things to him about me prophetically, which were true. Amazingly, one in particular he exclaimed out loud several times, "I see a centurion!" to which I laughed in joyful agreement. After the prayer was over, I explained to him that I occasionally preach wearing centurion's armor and had seen the Matthew 8 centurion in a vision. Dale Karoff's prophetic insight was a pleasant confirmation.

In Ephesians 6, the apostle Paul writes about a centurion's armor as a symbol of the instruments of spiritual warfare. It is well worth considering the symbolism of the pieces of armor to instruct us on their use in spiritual warfare. Paul was imprisoned under appeal to the Roman Emperor, most likely Nero at the time. He had been falsely accused and imprisoned in Judea. He was later taken on a precarious journey by sea, after leaving Herod's palace on the Mediterranean coast, and was personally guarded by the friendly centurion, Julias, to whom he was bound in chains (see Acts 27:1-3). Paul knew well what a centurion looked like and what he was capable of doing. Perhaps this man was a member of the elite "Italian cohort" assigned to settle some of the political and religious rumblings in Judea. Paul was maintained under house arrest in Rome and accompanied by centurions or legionnaires.

Paul was trained formally as a Pharisee, and he knew the Hebrew Scriptures well. He likely expanded Ephesians 6 around a similar passage from the prophet Isaiah:

> ...The Lord looked and was displeased that there was no justice. He saw that there was no one, He was appalled that there was no one to intervene; so His own arm worked salvation for Him, and His own righteousness sustained Him. He put on

*righteousness as His breastplate, and the **helmet of salvation** on His head; He put on the garments of vengeance and wrapped Himself in zeal as in a cloak. According to what they have done, so will He repay wrath to His enemies and retribution to His foes; He will repay the islands their due* (Isaiah 59:15-18, emphasis added).

The images of the breastplate of righteousness and the helmet of salvation are repeated nearly verbatim in Ephesians 6:14-17. We must first put on the *helmet of salvation*; without it none of the other armor is of any value. We must have salvation surrounding our minds, eyes, ears, mouths, and tongues. If salvation in Jesus does not impact what we think, see, hear, eat, and say, then do we really have the power of a transformed life in Him? Question yourself. The *breastplate of righteousness* needs to protect the life-giving core of our being. If we don't have righteousness, we only have "wrongeousness," and it is like having steel armor that is rusted, weak, and with holes that are large enough to let weapons pierce through and cause death.

The imagery of a sword is common in both the Old and New Testaments. God is portrayed as a warrior King in many places, and His servants are commanded to be sword-wielding loyalists. In Ephesians, the *double-edged sword* represents the Word of God (see Eph. 6:17; Heb. 4:12). However, most people incorrectly assume that Paul was referring to the written *logos* Word, when in fact he used the alternative term *rhema* Word of God, which is today's revelation from God. These word choices in Greek can be likened to the difference between past tense recorded words versus present tense or "now" words for today. Since it is a double-edged Roman gladius, it is an *offensive* thrusting weapon, the only offensive weapon mentioned in this chapter. It is used to attack the enemy at close range. Our adversary is a defeated, toothless lion who launches flaming arrows at us from the safe distance of a coward. But, we must go after him and attack him at close range using the sword, the rhema Word of God. The concept of direct revelation from God abounds in both the New Testament and the Old Testament (Hebrew) Scriptures. For instance, *"The Lord confides in those who fear Him; He makes His covenant known to them"* (Ps. 25:14). We can speculate that perhaps Paul used the term "double-edged" sword to indicate that we are to rely on both the *rhema* and the *logos* Word of God.

Paul's use of *rhema* is particularly relevant in the context of spiritual warfare. We must know the current plans revealed by God to defeat our enemy, not merely some historic way it was done in the past. Don't forget that our enemy is crafty and intelligent, knowing the written Word (logos) extremely well. The enemy can effectively use this knowledge as a weapon. The enemy is constantly changing his approach to each of us if in fact we're growing spiritually as a challenge to his authority. The freshness of the rhema revelation gives us distinct advantages over our foe, as God reveals the plans, strategies, and schemes of the enemy in our lives today. With this insight God provides countermeasures for us to pursue that are tailor-made to our assignment. "Now" rhema words can surprise our adversary and contravene his malicious plans.

It is important to note that rhema is directly related to prophetic revelatory understanding, spiritual discernment, and the blend of spiritual giftings granted to a believer. If you lack sensitivity to the prophetic promptings of the Holy Spirit, then you lack rhema revelation. It follows that you lack the ability to discern today the plans of the enemy (as provided by the Spirit), you can become easily deceived and defeated. If you lack rhema, you will be weak and ineffective when attempting to engage in spiritual warfare, even though you might have a considerable knowledge of the Bible. For example, there is a huge difference between merely knowing the *concept* about the discernment of demons influencing someone's body and soul (i.e., mind), after having read a story in the Bible, and actually doing it! The latter requires discerning and casting a demon out of someone. The mere head knowledge that someone else did it 2000 years ago pales in significance to actually having done it yourself aided by rhema revelation today. In addition, the lack of rhema insights may prove harmful to you, your family, and your associates when attempting to engage the enemy in certain areas of spiritual warfare. Learn to discern the "now" current voice of the Holy Spirit's promptings (a form of revelation) within your spirit, in which the Holy Spirit indwells all redeemed believers.

Remember that Jesus is portrayed as having a double-edged sword proceeding out of His mouth as a symbol of the power of His words (see Rev. 1:16; 19:15). When Jesus speaks, He wages war with satan and those aligned with the enemy in the heavenlies and the Earth. He uses us as His mouthpieces to declare on Earth those things He wants brought into alignment between the two realms, the natural Earth and the supernatural eternal world.

Matthew 6:9-13

The sword is our offensive weapon in spiritual warfare. We must be experienced with this weapon. It is curious to note that the small shepherd boy, David, used the weapon for which he had considerable experience. As David approached the Philistine giant Goliath, he didn't use the armor and weaponry that was suggested for him (see 1 Sam. 17). Rather, he picked up *five smooth stones,* and used one of them in his slingshot to bring down the giant. I've pondered those five smooth stones many times. They were smooth because they came from a stream, in which the flowing water polished the edges over many years. The Holy Spirit is often portrayed in the Scriptures as a stream or river. Thus, the Holy Spirit polishes the rough edges from our lives as we mature as disciples. The smooth surfaces represent a work of the *Holy Spirit,* whereas the hardness of the stones represents *Jesus,* the "solid rock." Just as the sword represents the rhema revelation of the Holy Spirit, so the smooth stones are weapons formed by the Holy Spirit's power for the right task.

Having in place the helmet of salvation, the breastplate of righteousness, and the sword of the Spirit (the rhema word of God), we must pick up the *shield of faith,* and use it as a defensive weapon. It is effective at blocking the flaming arrows of the enemy. Flaming arrows are effective in two ways: They damage the site that is directly pierced, and then the flames spread to other areas. A "little" sin can eventually produce a flaming inferno of destruction, reaching far beyond the initial problem. Faith in operation (i.e., risk-taking belief in action) is the tool that our Commander in Chief desires for us to have to protect against the weapons of the enemy. As we move forward in faith attacking the enemy, our faith shield will protect us from harm. If we don't have genuine faith, then the enemy will attack with a volley of "sin arrows" and we will be harmed.

We should be adorned and surrounded by a *belt of truth*. This Roman leather belt is a symbol of honor, and ironically provides only a minimal level of protection to the upper thighs and groin area. Truth is always a good thing, but it must also be accompanied by love (see 1 Cor. 13). We must learn to always speak the truth, but to also be careful to demonstrate love in our words and actions. On many occasions, truth needs to be tempered by compassion and understanding, but not always (e.g., when some prophetic warnings are spoken). Remember that El Elyon is always truthful, as He is the Father of all truth, whereas our enemy is the father of lies.

Brothers and sisters, if you do not walk in the truth, knowing that Jesus said that He is the truth (see Jn. 14:6), then you are not walking close to Him. You are listening to the voice of a stranger. Our world is very messed up, and it is commonplace to elevate lies and deception as entertaining and honorable. This must not be true of us.

> To the Jews who had believed Him, Jesus said, "If you hold to My teaching, you are really My disciples. Then you will know the **truth**, and the **truth** will set you free." They answered Him, "We are Abraham's descendants and have never been slaves of anyone. How can You say that we shall be set free?" Jesus replied, "I tell you the **truth**, everyone who sins is a slave to sin" (John 8:31-34, emphasis added).

When we listen to Yeshua the Jewish Messiah and the words of the Torah, we are hearing absolute truth in a pure form.

Paul's examples of pieces of a centurion's armor and weaponry provide us with insights for living today in a victorious manner. Let us follow the instructions of the apostle Paul and grow up! Let us use all the pieces of armor and weaponry that God provides and voluntarily engage in spiritual warfare.

INTENSE FAITH OF THE CANAANITE WOMAN

Jesus commended another foreigner for having intense faith as well. The Canaanite woman requested that her daughter be delivered of a demon (see Mt. 15:21-28). The Canaanite woman, like the centurion, was considered as a Gentile outsider to the Jews. The foreigners were despised and to be avoided according to religious custom. But, because of her persistence, humility, and understanding of Jesus' authority, her prayer was answered. He declared to her, "*Woman, you have **great faith**! Your request is granted*" (Mt. 15:28, emphasis added). She managed to redirect Jesus' priorities to answer her request, even though Jesus was not intending at that juncture to reach outside the "lost sheep of Israel" (i.e., the Jews).

We see a similar encounter of altering the clock by Jesus' own mother at the marriage feast at Cana (see Jn. 2:1-11). Jesus said, "*Dear woman, why do you involve Me?...My time has not yet come*" (Jn. 2:4). He wasn't planning to perform miracles yet, but her request redirected Jesus' priorities and timing. The examples from these two women, one a Canaanite Gentile and the other a Jew (coincidentally in Cana), reveal to us that Jesus listens to earnest requests, even when the timing might not be as He had preferred or planned. This is a key principle to effective intercession. That should encourage all of us to press into Him with our Holy Spirit-inspired prayers and petitions.

The example of the Canaanite woman also instructs us that He answers prayers of everyone. Gentiles and women were not necessarily held in high regard among the religious Jewish men of that day. So when Jesus answered the prayers of (1) a Gentile foreigner; (2) a woman; and (3) at the wrong time, isn't He making a profound statement to us today? Jesus is asking of His followers, "*What is the desire of your heart?*" God said that if we delight in Him as righteous followers, He will give us the desires of our heart (see Ps. 20; Ps. 37). May we begin to approach our Father in Heaven in greater

27

confidence, knowing that both Jesus and the Holy Spirit intercede before our heavenly Father on our behalf. May we demonstrate intense faith like that of the Roman centurion and the Canaanite woman.

Chapter One

QUESTIONS

1. When the centurion (see Mt. 8) approached Jesus about his servant's problem, what were some of the Roman soldier's possible concerns, fears, and risks?

2. Why does Jesus commend "childlike faith" and submission to authorities?

3. Can you "kick against the goads" or "buck authority" and have God's anointing and favor continually resting upon you?

4. Centurions are noted throughout the New Testament and examples are found in the Gospels and the Book of Acts. Were the Roman centurions "good" or "bad" in each encounter with Jesus or His disciples, such as Paul?

5. Define the difference between *logos* and *rhema* Word of God.

6. Who are the authorities in your life? List them and score yourself concerning whether the relationship is in biblical alignment or rebellion. Do any of these relationships need correction or improvement?

   a. Family (e.g., husbands and parents)

   b. Government (e.g., police and elected officials)

   c. Work

   d. Church universal and local church

   e. Community organizations, committees, and boards

Chapter Two

WHAT IS GENUINE FAITH?

Without faith it is impossible to please God, because anyone who comes to Him must believe that He exists and that He rewards those who earnestly seek Him (Hebrews 11:6).

Once while accompanying my dad on a stroll through Mt. Vernon Cemetery, south of my hometown of Atchison, Kansas, we were reading the inscriptions of some tombstones. We encountered the grave of John J. Ingalls, a former senator during the 19th century. He wrote *In Praise of Blue Grass* and included the following thought-provoking insight, some of which was chiseled into his tombstone, "*When...the foolish wrangle of the market and forum is closed, grass heals over the scar which our descent into the bosom of the earth has made, and the carpet of the infant becomes the blanket of the dead.*" When the memory of our passing through this life-giving planet is noted merely by the soil and grass above our remains, will we have any regrets? And more importantly, will God be pleased with us?

Central to this important question is: Do we choose to live primarily to please *ourselves*, to please *others*, or to please the one true living *God*? We have the choice as long as we have breath to primarily please only one of the three answers (i.e., ourselves, others, or God). Will we give our days to meeting the desires of ourselves in the pursuit of personal happiness and pleasures? Will we, out of fear of man, seek to please others in view of what they might think or say about us? Or, will we give our best to be pleasing to El Shaddai?

Hebrews 11:6 should be a wake-up call to all of us. The path to acceptance in the eyes of the sovereign Almighty God is a very narrow path. But, He has graciously provided us with this key insight. By following the path of *faith* we are considered as pleasing to Him. So, this raises another question: If faith is the requirement, then shouldn't we know what genuine faith is and what it is not? It would be foolish to live our lives assuming that we had that definition down correctly, when in fact we had missed the mark. If we misunderstand what genuine faith is, then we also miss the blessings inherent within it.

Our spiritual Father God (the intimate Daddy—Abba) is seeking worshipers who will be in *relationship* with Him, and thus be pleasing to Him, above all other things that they pursue in life. Recall that pleasing God is the focus of the first several teachings of the Ten Commandments given to Moses after leaving Egypt into the desert. This concept is central to a proper understanding of our relationship as the "created" to our Creator. The first several requirements of the Ten Commandments can be concisely paraphrased as—God Almighty commands us to be in an exclusive, yielded, and loving relationship with Himself. He tells us through Hebrews chapter 11 that faith is one of the most important ingredients that we must demonstrate in our lives in order for Him to be pleased with us. The preeminent position of faith is reinforced elsewhere by, "*The only thing that counts is faith expressing itself through love*" (Gal. 5:6, emphasis added).

DEFINING SAVING FAITH

In the New Testament Greek, the term "faith" is the noun *pistis*, and is related to the verb *pisteuo*. The words mean to trust or believe, and typically anticipate action in accordance with the belief. Biblical faith has one predominant meaning (i.e., risk-taking belief in action), which we will discuss in greater detail after we first briefly consider "saving faith."

When we possess Jesus' gift of salvation it is sometimes referred to as having "faith," when in fact it is something special and an exception to the general rule. "Saving faith" is aligning our will in

Matthew 28:19 The Trinity mentioned together

repentance to trust in Jesus for salvation of our eternal spirits. This is accomplished by voluntarily accepting the death and resurrection of Jesus the Christ (or Yeshua the Messiah or Anointed One), in our place for our own sins. Through God's gracious and precious gift of His Son Jesus, we can enter into a new relationship through "saving faith." Our new birth through Jesus' actions provides forgiveness before God the Father in the throne room in the heavenly realm. According to the New Testament, without repentance and relationship, we'll never know God. When viewed externally, salvation is "merely" the alignment of our mind and spirit to accept the completed work of Jesus on the cross. It is quite simple, as the recipient of saving grace doesn't do much of anything, other than repent of sin and agree with God's written Word. Typically (at that time or following), an individual who has voluntarily received the free gift of salvation publicly demonstrates their acknowledgement of this internal spiritual change by the external symbol of water baptism (see 1 Pet. 3:18-22; Mt. 28:19; Rom. 6:1-7). The literal water of baptism does not change the individual's spirit, but it symbolizes his or her submission to the will of God. Water baptism is a symbol of the repenter's intentions to follow Jesus and to depart from his or her former patterns of sin.

Our eternal salvation through Jesus' death on the cross and resurrection is a result of His grace expressing itself through our faith. It is not something you can work for or obtain by merely being a "good" person (see Eph. 2:8-9). You can't obtain salvation by going to church or synagogue, following religious teachings, being "religious," or being declared or imputed as a Christian by someone else. It is not accomplished by anything that we can do ourselves, or that anyone else can do for us, with the exception of Jesus, who was and is perfect. We merely accept what He has done for us and place our trust in God's provision through Jesus. We are redeemed by the blood of the Lamb, a Hebraic picture of the Passover during Moses' days, and then subsequently with symbolic relevance to the crucified Jesus. There is *nothing* that we do to earn redemption and salvation by our own good deeds. Good deeds serve a good purpose, but

Good to Read at Baptisms Romans 6:1-7

they are of no value in obtaining salvation, which starts the relationship. Good deeds should *follow* after repentance.

However, we are strongly admonished to not treat the free gift of salvation lightly. We are to *"continue to work out our salvation with fear and trembling"* (Phil. 2:12). We are to demonstrate genuine fear of the Lord in our attitudes and actions. We are to demonstrate spiritual *fruit* in keeping with our repentance. We must be righteous and holy to be in relationship with Him (see Ezek. 18). Sadly, the fear of the Lord is no longer a trendy topic to preach about, as it was in the days of the early American awakener, Jonathan Edwards. He delivered in his famous sermon in 1741 entitled "Sinners in the Hand of an Angry God," that our lives on Earth are maintained by a thin veneer of God's grace over a pit of hellish eternity, and that men and women easily and naturally slip into a Godless eternity if they do not voluntarily enter into a personal relationship with Jesus. Our Western "churchianity" no longer wants to hear about the God of severity and harsh consequences for sin, rather they only want the "God of love." The reason that we received our expensive salvation by Jesus is to obey and honor Him. It wasn't just for our own self-serving convenience. Our obedience will enable us to be victorious overcomers at the end of the race, as we're repeatedly admonished in the Book of Revelation of Jesus, which was given through the apostle and prophet John.

The Hebrew name for Jesus is Yeshua, or in the English-speaking Western world, Joshua. That name means "salvation," and provides further explanation of the intended purposes of Jesus' life, as declared by an angelic visitor to Mary and Joseph prior to conception (see Lk. 1:31; Mt. 1:21). Just as Joshua, the Old Testament prototype, delivered the Hebrews into the Promised Land after Moses' death, so Jesus delivers His followers into the "land" of His new Kingdom. As His name infers, Jesus was, is, and will be our salvation. Through faith, Jesus is bringing us into a covenant relationship out of the old and into the new, just as Joshua before Him brought the newly born Hebrew nation into a new land and covenant relationship following the death of Moses. Whenever we speak the name of Jesus, we are declaring salvation over our lives and circumstances!

The name of Jesus is a name with a special meaning, chosen for Him by His heavenly Father, not by His natural father Joseph of Nazareth. The angel of the Lord visited and declared to Joseph, "*...you are to give Him the name **Yeshua**, because He will **save** His people from their sins*" (Mt. 1:21, emphasis added). Since Yeshua means "salvation," note the intentional redundancy of His *name* and His *purpose* before He was even born! The angel of the Lord also repeated the words of the prophet Isaiah declaring another name for Jesus, "*They will call Him Immanuel—which means, God with us*" (Mt. 1:23). Of all the possible names that could have been chosen, God Almighty chose the special name Yeshua (Jesus) because of its meaning, even though it was a common name in those days in Jewish Judea and Galilee. Have you chosen Yeshua as the supreme named God over all of your life? Has He become your personal salvation and your personal Immanuel, God living with you and in you by the indwelling Holy Spirit? If not, please do so now. You will not be disappointed.

FAITH = RISK-TAKING BELIEF IN ACTION

Having mentioned above the meaning of saving faith, let us turn our attention to the common meaning of faith in the Bible, which will be the primary focus of this book. This is the usual type or form of faith mentioned throughout the Bible. It requires something that saving faith does not. The common type of genuine faith requires us to do something in action. It is not passive. It is not something done for us (i.e., as in Jesus' gift of salvation) that we simply accept; it is something we must engage in through our own actions.

Confusion is common about the definition of faith. Many opinions are incorrect, vague, imprecise, or non-biblical—even among those who consider themselves believers in Jesus. In error they often consider mere "belief" as being the same as "faith." Belief is a mental process whereby we agree in our minds with a concept, teaching, fact, or opinion. Beliefs do not necessarily require any actions. Beliefs can be passive and often are. Beliefs can be held in high regard and fiercely defended within our minds, yet without changing us or prompting us to actions.

People believe in all sorts of things both true and false, for instance: a newspaper report of an event that they didn't witness; a bad report about someone overheard during gossip; words spoken by a politician; what a chemistry teacher taught about atoms without ever actually seeing a real molecule up close; various superstitions, such as UFOs from outer space; the teachings of New Age religious gurus; diet fads; Santa Claus; the "tooth fairy"; that Nirvana is achieved through attaining great wealth; and, that we'll always face death and taxes. However, even though people may hold a certain belief, they might not take even a single action in their lives that would be consistent with that belief, regardless of whether it is true or not. They merely believe it, but don't act upon it. Belief without action is not faith.

Genuine faith requires action! The second form of faith, the common definition, requires actions by us in accordance with our beliefs. Most of the time the Bible refers to this kind of faith. Genuine Faith has three essential ingredients:

- *It* must be something that is unseen!
- I must believe that *it* is true for me!
- I must walk towards *it*!

When all three principles are working in unison, we demonstrate genuine faith. Belief in the unseen operating in action is genuine faith. The Book of Hebrews tells us that we can have faith only in that which is currently unseen by our eyes of sight. The author wrote, "*Now faith is being sure of what we hope for and certain of what we do not see. This is what the ancients were commended for. By faith we understand that the universe was formed at God's command, so that what is seen was not made out of what was visible*" (Heb. 11:1-3, emphasis added). Faith is the unswerving belief in action that is focused on something that we can't see in the natural from our current position. It is like perceiving or believing that there is a treasure in the next valley that is concealed by a mountain directly in front of you. You can't see a single molecule of the treasure from where you are standing. You must believe that the unseen treasure exists, and then walk toward the mountain to initiate genuine faith. As long as you just believe that there's a treasure in the next valley, it isn't faith. Honestly, the belief won't do you any good until action is taken. Faith begins when we start to walk forward toward the goal. Furthermore, Paul admonishes us, "*So we fix our eyes not on what is seen, but on what is **unseen**. For what is seen is temporary, but what is **unseen** is eternal*" (2 Cor. 4:18, emphasis added).

Our family has an acquaintance, Mike Diffee in Birmingham, who is entirely blind. Yet, he has developed capabilities that few sighted individuals have mastered because they are too heavily dependent on sight as their primary navigation tool. Two skills in particular are quite interesting to observe. Mike cannot see anything, yet he can determine the distance to walls by listening with his ears to echoes, similar to echo location used by bats with high frequencies. Using his ears he can estimate where he is in relationship to his surroundings. As a daring child he would ride a bicycle on the street using only the sounds of someone near him on another bike or car to guide him. In the physical realm Mike can "see," but without using eyes. This sight-impaired man can also speak in reverse phonetics, like "back-masking." He can listen to a sentence, and then speak it backwards in anti-sense phonetics. If you record him speaking in this manner on a tape and then play it backwards, you then hear the sentence in normal language. Our blind friend Mike is remarkable in these two oddities, which he has mastered. However, he is a living example of a physical metaphor of seeing into the unseen realm. Just as blind Mike has developed his abilities to "see" the natural realm using his other senses and mental abilities, we need to develop the ability over time to discern where God is leading us by faith.

If you have not ever sought out a blind or deaf individual to befriend, I highly recommend it. My beautiful daughter, Catherine, has voluntarily learned to use sign language with her hands, arms, and facial expressions so that she can be of assistance to hearing-impaired individuals, whom she occasionally encounters. When I watch her worshiping God while signing during songs of praise, I am moved emotionally, and occasionally to the point of tears. She has an ability to speak in a form that few of us even comprehend. Yet, this serves as another physical metaphor for being able to speak without phonetics—another parallel into see-ing into the unseen realm. Faith is not dependent on our natural neurological senses of sight, hearing, touch, taste, or smell. Faith is not dependent on our intellect or ability to reason. Faith goes beyond our senses and understanding into the unseen realm.

I respect Reinhard Bonnke, the hardworking founder of Christ for All Nations. He is considered by many people to be the world's most successful evangelist over the past decade, at least in numeri-cal terms. God's anointing in power is upon him to work miracles and influence nations, especially within Africa. Reinhard often preaches live to audiences of approximately one million people at a single place and time. Since 1987 I have expected that in my own life God will use me to minister to the nations in ways that might resemble Reinhard's ministry in part. I see him as a model disciple of Jesus to emulate in my own life.

Mr. Bonnke wrote in his book entitled *Faith: The Link with God's Power*, "People often say, 'I'll believe it when I see it.' No they won't. They can't. You can only believe or have faith in what you don't see." Once they have seen it, then it is established as fact and there is no room for belief any longer. In the same book, Reinhard also notes that, "Faith is like a lamp; it is of no use in daylight." Faith permits us to see spiritually in the dark or unseen realm.

Remember the story of Samuel as he presumed that he was to anoint the wrong eldest son of Jesse, Eliab, instead of the youngest son, David. The Lord said, *"Do not consider his appearance or his height, for I have rejected him. The Lord does not look at the things man looks at. Man looks at the outward appearance, but the Lord looks at the heart"* (1 Sam. 16:7). Faith requires us to see beyond the limitations of our own eyes or cultural norms, and to precisely discern the will of God. When we operate in faith, we become more like Him. Just as the Lord doesn't see only the outward natural appearance, so we, too, should grow in the ability to see from a heavenly perspective.

FAITH IS DIFFICULT FOR INTELLECTUALS

As a scientist with the ability to be critical and judgmental in analysis, I conclude that genuine faith is irrational and illogical, at least up to the point where the faith produces some visible result. God looks to us to exercise faith in Him and His power, but that expectation by Him is unreasonable from our perspective. Action based on belief in the unseen realm is not logical until we observe the consequences of an act of faith. For instance, it was illogical for Abraham to believe in advance that he and his elderly infertile wife would produce a child, but he believed and acted in faith. But, once this married couple realized the consequence of faith as Isaac was conceived and born, their confidence in God was bolstered. Thus, it established a testimony or evidence that faith really works. Therefore, if you examine the possibilities in advance of risk-taking action, it will almost invariably seem illogical and unreasonable, until the act of obedience has been performed. *Obedience is the real test of faith!* Obedience and faith are almost synonymous terms. Once the testimony is established, our faith is built up further. Yet, many of us have the tendency toward security, whereby we say we'll build something only after we have all the money in the bank. Once all the money is in the bank, it takes no faith to build it. Building without money takes faith.

We must train ourselves to see with the eyes of faith and not trust the physical eyes of sight, as circumstances alone would dictate. Faith is not genuine if it is dependent on our circumstances. Faith looks beyond our circumstances. *Circumstances are the fire extinguishers of faith!* Difficult circumstances can produce fear, and often paralyzing fear that stops us from moving forward in action (see Mk. 4:16-17). When our thoughts about tough circumstances become fully entrenched in our minds, we become firmly deceived by the *spirit of unbelief*, which can involve demonic influences in extreme cases. But, God has not given us a spirit of timidity or fear (see 2 Tim. 1:7).

We must see beyond the circumstances hindering our trust in the Lord. Coupled with hard circumstances are our natural tendencies toward fear, worry, and brooding. Ask yourself this question, "Are you worried about anything that happened three thousand years ago?" Certainly not! Neither is God Almighty, who operates in timelessness. He is not worried about anything in the past, and for that matter in the present or future. Since in His sovereignty He sees everything from *end-to-beginning*, He's not worried, and neither should we be. When we appropriate His faith within us, we tap into His confident, eternal, fearless, and timeless perspective. Now ask yourself a second question, "Can a dead man be raised to life today *after* he has died? We all agree that's one tough circumstance! But, faith enabled Jesus to see beyond the natural timeline, with its imposing difficulties, to raise people from the dead. I believe in resurrection power wholeheartedly, and I desire to see people raised from the dead myself through His faith. If you weren't aware of it, there are a growing number of reliable testimonies of God raising people from the dead today through the actions of men and women of faith (and mostly in the Third World). Nothing is too difficult for Him.

Not only can unpleasant difficult circumstances be a source of hindrance to faith, but so can pleasant and comfortable circumstances be a stumbling block to faith (see Mk. 4:18-19). We can be tripped up satan by either discomfort or comfort!

This is especially true of individuals living in the affluence of the Western world. A missionary to a Third World country once said to me that the peoples of impoverished nations spend the majority of their time just trying to supply for their family's minimal daily needs (e.g., water, food, clothing, and simple shelter), whereas American and European Christians spend the majority of their time pursuing the pleasures, comforts, and luxuries of life and only a small portion of their time actually meeting fundamental needs. Those of us living in the West have a very difficult time discerning the difference between our "wants" and our "needs." It is as if we have become blinded by the comforts and luxuries of life. Please don't let the fires of faith be extinguished by circumstances, either bad or good. When we see only with the *eyes of sight,* the flames of faith will not burn within us. When we fail to see by the *eyes of faith,* we are not pleasing to God.

It is of no value to be aware of something that is unseen without personalizing or appropriating it for yourself. Let's imagine we hear a trusted friend saying, "I know based on valuable firsthand information that if you invest in this stock in company X, you're going to receive a great return on investment within six months...I just know it." However, unlike our friend who acted upon his or her beliefs and reaped the reward, we just acknowledged in our minds that, "Yes, it is true" based on our trust in his or her words, but we did not make the investment necessary to reap our reward. Faith requires that we consider it to be true for ourselves. The exact same situation can produce genuine faith in one individual, while others look on, ponder it, fail to take action, and miss out. The individual with faith receives the blessing, while the others receive nothing. Furthermore, in some cases individuals go beyond not acting on it to declaring that it is false. They turn a potential blessing for themselves into a curse. A blessing rejected can be the same thing as a curse.

We must complete the three conditions—not only see with the eyes of faith into the unseen, and believe it for ourselves, but we must walk toward it. In the example mentioned above, we would need to write a check and invest our own money in the stock of that company in speculation based upon the "word" from our trusted friend. That would be risk-taking, genuine faith. We would have no certainty that our investment would ultimately succeed, but we place our trust, actions, and money on the line based on our belief, albeit prompted by our trusted friend. Let us not lose sight of the fact that our trusted friend is Jesus who after His resurrection sent "another" Counselor/Comforter to us, the Holy Spirit to prompt us to action in faith. The Holy Spirit speaks today in the written logos Word of God and via rhema revelation to His children. The Holy Spirit also uses other fellow disciples of Jesus to prompt us to take faith steps. We can learn from their examples and instruction.

As a public demonstration while preaching, I occasionally will hold up a small amount of money, such as a one dollar note (or a ten Rupee note in India), declaring to the audience, "In my hand is a dollar bill. You may have it. Who would like to take it?" After a few moments of intense curiosity, a brave soul will then raise his or her hand, albeit with trepidation as he or she doesn't know whether this is an embarrassing trick or not. I'll call him or her forward and hand the individual the bill. The recipient is then complimented for a tiny amount of courage, in which he or she takes possession of the gift that has been offered. I then ask everyone, "Did it take *faith* for him or her to receive this money?" Many in the crowd often reply "Yes," but they are shocked at my reply...they are wrong. It takes *no* faith to accept this gift, as the recipient can clearly see it in advance. There is no room for faith when you see it directly in front of you.

Then, I hold up an *empty* hand and declare, "In my hand is a dollar bill. You may have it. Who would like to take it?" Now this produces even greater anxiety and tension than before, as I'm making a statement by faith to the audience. Giggles of discomfort are often heard. Many are looking to their left and right to see what the others will do, not sure if they should be the first to act. Often the crowd needs to be prodded for a long while before someone with courage will venture to raise his or her hand and come forward. Once he or she touches my seemingly empty hand, I smile and commend them with extravagant praise. I make an example of them and open my wallet to reward them with not only the anticipated dollar bill, but also more money that they hadn't even anticipated. The recipient is praised loudly for not only taking the risk of courage in the face of possible public embarrassment before hundreds or thousands of staring people, but because he or she has demonstrated genuine faith by coming forward based upon my words (and reputation). The person has merely trusted the preacher's words without seeing with the eyes of sight. In most cases I am a stranger to most or all of the people in the audience; they don't know how reliable I am or whether I'm setting them up for an embarrassment. Our faith must operate in a similar manner in order to be pleasing to God. We, too, need to stand up and touch the seemingly "empty" hand of the invisible God. We need to have childlike faith and trust Him to provide.

Do you recognize the profound irony of this message on faith being delivered by a Ph.D. scientist, well trained in molecular and cellular biology for over 11 years at three well-known institutions, and who has served as a professor in two universities and founder of scientific corporations? Who better to deliver a message on seeing into the unseen realm of faith than someone who is trained by education, career, and profession to never trust anything that can't be proven scientifically by the eyes of sight? To many people the example of my profession *vis-à-vis* my strong faith in the God of the Bible is an oxymoron. It is illogical to most college-educated people living in the Western world, where Greco-Roman dependence on knowledge and science reigns supreme. Faith does not come easily to a trained scientist, and especially a "life scientist" (e.g., biologist), as some of the teaching and dogma is philosophically opposed to Judeo-Christianity.

The majority of scientists I know are practical agnostics or atheists or they have adopted a form of liberal theistic religion that permits them great flexibility to do as they please with their morality, ethics, and values. Most scientists appear to have established themselves as the ultimate judge and arbiter of so-called "truth," which they usually limit to "facts" and conclusions about "facts or theories." You will rarely find an exception among professional scientists in Western universities, as their education, training, and patterns of thought strongly reinforce this principle. It reminds me of a TV program several decades ago about a policeman who would always use the same dispassionate line to someone he was questioning, "Just the facts, sir." Many scientists and intellectuals doubt that "absolute truth" from a perspective outside of themselves is a concept that is reliable. But, there is a huge difference between "facts" and the "truth."

These skeptical scientists remind me of a similar remark spoken by Pontius Pilate, the Roman Governor over Judea during the early first century, who questioned Jesus, "*What is truth?*" (Jn. 18:38, emphasis added), in response to Jesus' words during His trial, "*You are right in saying I am a king. In fact, for this reason I was born, and for this I came into the world, to testify to the truth. Everyone on the side of truth listens to Me*" (Jn. 18:37, emphasis added). Remember that the apostle John informs us that Jesus *is* the Word of God and the *truth* of God (see Jn. 1:1-18,14:6, emphasis added). Our God uses the foolish things of this world to confound the wise, as He declared,

> *"I will destroy the wisdom of the wise; the intelligence of the intelligent I will frustrate." Where is the wise man? Where is the scholar? Where is the philosopher of this age? Has not God made foolish the wisdom of the world? For since in the wisdom of God the world through its wisdom did not know Him, God was pleased through the foolishness of what was preached to save those who believe. Jews demand miraculous signs and Greeks [Gentiles] look for wisdom, but we preach Christ crucified: a stumbling block to the Jews and foolishness to the Gentiles...But God chose the foolish things of the world to shame the wise; God chose the weak things of the world to shame the strong. He chose the lowly things of this world and the despised things—and the things that are not— to nullify the things that are, so that no one may boast before him* (1 Corinthians 1:19-23,27-29).

No intellectual may approach God based on his or her own intellect and be pleasing in God's sight. For we do not define the sovereign God; He defines us. We do not make the rules of the natural and spiritual universes; He does. *"The man without the Spirit does not accept the things that come from the Spirit of God, for they are foolishness to him, and he cannot understand them, because they are spiritually discerned"* (1 Cor. 2:14). It is my observation that very few scientists and intellectuals have entered into a relationship with the true living God, for, *"God is spirit, and His worshipers must worship in spirit and in truth"* (Jn. 4:24).

The brightest minds on the planet do not enter into His presence easily, for we must become like children in humility to be pleasing to Him. Jesus declared, *"I praise You, Father, Lord of heaven and earth, because You have hidden these things from the wise and learned, and revealed them to little children"* (Mt. 11:25). He spoke further, *"I tell you the truth, unless you change and become like little children, you will never enter the kingdom of heaven. Therefore, whoever humbles himself like this child is the greatest in the kingdom of heaven"* (Mt. 18:3-4). Children demonstrate trust as the dependents of their superiors. It is impossible to know God without humbly submitting to His authority. Pride is the "bread-and-butter" of an intellectual's thought life, and pride is the enemy of humility that is needed to approach God on favorable terms.

This is the same reason why the highly educated rabbinic Pharisees, Sadducees, and scribes had such great difficulty in coming to Jesus in humility (see Mt. 23; Lk. 11:37-54). Knowledge puffs up our heads with pride (see 1 Cor. 8:1), and pride precludes us from having an audience with the King, for He is opposed to the proud. It is a surprise to many Christians that great knowledge of the Bible does not make a way to God for us, if we are relying on our own mental understanding. Esteem for knowledge of the Bible alone can produce "bibliolatry," idolizing knowledge of the Bible rather than worshiping the Author of the Bible. Herein is an inherent and strong warning about education in a seminary! You can have a college degree in biblical studies and yet not be in a genuine relationship with the Author of the Bible. Jesus said to the religious leaders of His day, "*And the Father who sent Me has Himself testified concerning Me. You have never heard His voice nor seen His form, nor does His word dwell in you, for you do not believe the one He sent [i.e., Jesus]. You diligently study the Scriptures because you think that by them you possess eternal life. These are the Scriptures that testify about Me, yet you refuse to come to Me to have life*" (Jn. 5:37-40). The unyielded mind is a great hindrance to genuine faith, even if one possesses plenty of Bible knowledge, which was certainly true of the rabbis and teachers of Jesus' day. It is extremely important that we understand—it is about *obedience* to the knowledge of biblical truth, not merely having knowledge of biblical truth! There are far too many casualties in Judeo-Christianity caused by the pursuit and possession of knowledge alone, even among well-intentioned individuals.

Have you heard it said by a skeptical intellectual agnostic or atheist, who declares in mocking and defiant rhetoric, "Faith in Jesus is merely *a crutch for the weak*"? The critics deserve a compliment for this accusation. The skeptics are in large part correct. If you don't come to God Almighty in weakness, you can't come to Him at all. For, "*God opposes the proud but gives grace to the humble*" (Jas. 4:6; see also Prov. 3:34; Prov. 16:5; Mt. 23:12). Weakness and humility as its evidence are requirements. But, the skeptic's accusation is not entirely correct. He or she should go even further in his or her derogatory sentiment. It isn't just a crutch; faith in Jesus is everything! It is an entire life support system, consisting of lungs, eyes, heart, brain, etc.

An unyielded mind is a dangerous weapon. I know many scientists, intellectuals, and professors around the world, and even have had conversations with several Nobel Prize recipients, yet I have seldom observed any evidence of biblical faith in the unseen eternal God in any of them. It is very rare indeed. The intellect, mind, and emotions can place many roadblocks in the path to genuine faith. We must come humbly and in faith expecting Him to be the rewarder of those who earnestly seek after Him (see Heb. 11:6). If we come in pride, we won't find Him and He won't reveal Himself to us (see Ps. 18:25-29). We'll just create a god and theology in our minds of our own liking that suits the condition of our bankrupt morality and limited understanding. May this not be true of us. Rather, may we be careful to discern the strategies of the enemy as he uses intellectuals within colleges, universities, seminaries, and the business world to deceive the populous.

If you find your inner spirit stirred by some of the "less-than-sugar-coated" words that you have just read, please reconsider the *truth* of these remarks. Our God is a merciful and compassionate God, quick to listen and slow to avenge. Please place your trust in Him, and not in yourself. May we always approach God on His terms that include living intentionally in the faith realm, and not merely in the knowledge realm.

A life of faith operates in opposition to the natural world in which believers find themselves living as "aliens." The rules of the natural world often run counter to the desires of the Holy Spirit residing within believers. In the *Matrix* films a battle is waged within a seemingly real physical world, but it is nothing more than an elegant computer code serving as an alternative reality that masks the truth. There are some obvious parallels between the *Matrix* films and the conflict between the natural and spiritual worlds surrounding us. Both are realities, but only one of them has an eternal presence and ultimate value—the spiritual world. When we operate by the eyes of faith, we grow in our understanding of the spiritual world that is governed by God Almighty. But, a portion of what we encounter in the physical realm is manipulated by satan, the father of lies. The devil has been granted some authority over the Earth, and his influence is felt in all of our lives. When we tap into the spiritual world by genuine faith, we have the ability via our relationship with the living true God, to effect changes in the spiritual realm which often translates into actions in the physical realm. Without faith, we lack a valuable "weapon" to fight against the devil and his schemes to steal, kill, and destroy. Therefore, let us take actions in risk-taking belief. Without faith, we will not be pleasing to God. In the simplest of terms—faith equals obedience to God's revelation.

CONSEQUENCES OF NOT LIVING BY FAITH

If God's revealed truth concerning our individual obligations to exercise faith in order to be pleasing to God does not stir up action within us, then consider briefly the consequences of not exercising risk-taking belief in action. Without faith we miss intended blessings and opportunities to advance the Kingdom of God. Doing His will is exciting, fulfilling, and risky business. While we're "aliens" on assignment here on Earth, we can choose to participate in God's intended wonderful plans to plunder hell's domain, thus releasing captives and lifting up the oppressed. Failure to please God by our actions also means failure to reach His intended destiny for our own selves and those with whom we have some influence in the here and now.

Not only is a faith-less life displeasing to our Father in Heaven while we're still here on Earth, but consider another motivator— **HELL IS REAL!** Hell is more real than the ground we walk upon and the air we breathe. Hell is more real than the worst horror film or book ever imaged in the minds of mankind. Hell is worse than the Holocaust of World War II, in which millions of European Jews were systematically and mercilessly murdered by anti-Semitic loyalists. Hell is worse than the genocidal massacres in Uganda, Rwanda, Sudan, the Ivory Coast, and Cambodia. Hell is worse that the most grotesque physical ailment on Earth. Hell is worse the most rotten prisons of the Third World, in which prisoners are treated worse than dogs.

God has clearly spoken to me that I am compelled to declare to everyone, and especially to those who have ears to hear, *"Tell them, hell is real!"* This horrible reality is inescapable. Jesus Himself spoke of hell as a horrible reality (see Lk. 16:19-31). It is foolish to think otherwise. You have been fed a bucket of lies, if you think that upon death everyone goes to a heavenly bliss regardless of whether they follow Jesus the Crucified as their Savior and Lord. Only Jesus is *the* Way, *the* Truth, and *the* Life (see Jn. 14:6). Through His crucified body and resurrection, we gain access to Heaven. Alternatively, you have been fed a bucket of lies, if you think that upon death everyone merely perishes into nothingness!

The absolute reality of an eternal hell (and Heaven) will be observed by every single human being after they die, and even by a subset of people before death. This truth is inescapable and uncomfortable...and it should be! Our El Shaddai, all-sufficient God, does not delight in the death and eternal punishment of anyone (see Ezek. 18). He desires that we all repent of sin and accept His terms to enter an eternal relationship with Him. It is our own individual choice. Only a fool would accept an eternity in hell if he or she understood the reality of that God-forsaken horrible place. It is a place of total darkness with no photons of light, like the darkest of any cave on Earth. Since God is light, where He is absent there is no light. Hell is a place of torture, horrible sounds, excruciating temperatures and odors, and unfathomable tormenting experiences. This horrible place is even feared by our enemy, the devil and his subordinates. They don't want to be there, either. Satan isn't looking forward to being sent into the eternal lake of burning sulfur, which is his ultimate state (see Rev. 20:7-15). The devil wouldn't choose to go there, rather he will be *sent* there by God Almighty as a consequence of his rebellion. Listen folks, satan is the ultimate loser! You, too will be an eternal loser if you choose to follow him into hell, rather than repenting and clinging onto the blood-stained robe of the crucified Jesus Christ.

Too many people react against the truth of the existence of hell. They desire to deny it, or diminish it, or replace it with an alternative concept. My friends, I plead with you do not misunderstand this truth—*hell is real!*

Chapter Two

QUESTIONS

1. Do you agree that genuine faith means "risk-taking belief in action"? If not, suggest an alternative definition.

2. Which *women* in the Bible do you most appreciate for their faith? (This might be a bit of a stretch for some males, who are inexperienced or inconsiderate of this role reversal.)

3. Which individual in the Bible would your close friends and family say you most resemble? Ask them. It might reveal to you some of your own strengths and weaknesses.

4. What risks do you recognize in accepting Jesus as Savior and Lord? What are the risks of not doing so?

5. When your life is over and you appear before Jesus on bended knee as everyone shall, on what basis will your life be judged? Will you have a defense for your life and a justification for your sins?

6. What has been the single hardest thing you have had to do "in faith"?

7. If you could literally experience the realities of both Heaven and hell today in a pair of visions from God, how would that impact your faith?

8. Do you believe in a literal *Heaven* (see Rev. 4, 5, 21-22)? If so, what are the requirements for eternal residence there?

9. Do you believe in a literal *hell* (see Rev. 20)? If so, what are the requirements for eternal residence there?

Chapter Three

ENTREPRENEURS AND THE RISK-REWARD RELATIONSHIP

The kingdom of heaven is like treasure hidden in a field. When a man found it, he hid it again, and then in his joy went and sold all he had and bought that field (Matthew 13:44).

A small subset of people find it relatively easy to take risks in certain areas, even extreme risks, whereas most people find it frightening to venture out in a new direction. For every risk taker there are considerably more security-conscious risk-averse individuals. For every genuine leader there are considerably more security-conscious risk-averse followers. A large part of this is inherent in our personalities that were developed *in utero* in our mother's womb and during early childhood development. It is as if some people are just hard-wired this way.

During the month immediately prior to our wedding in 1981, I participated in a clinical research study at the University of Kansas concerning the physiologic response to extreme stress. In this study, which was reported in the journal *Science* the following year, I was trained to jump out of an airplane at 3,000 feet while strapped to a portable EKG recorder. I jumped out of the plane. Fortunately they provided a parachute. The goal was to study the neurotransmitter molecules released in the subjects' urine samples before and after the stress-inducing jump...and hopefully not during! It takes faith to overcome the fear and anxiety of voluntarily doing something that is considered as highly risky or in this case potentially life threatening. In this example one needed to trust the instructor, the training techniques, the pilot, the plane, the main parachute, the reserve parachute, and the other gear. If any of these things failed, you would likely experience a casualty. However, the reward for jumping is exhilarating fun and a unique perspective and experience for a couple of minutes while floating down to *terra firma*.

In addition to parachuting, I've had my share of voluntary risky thrills in life, including skiing on water and snow, motorcycling, and hunting. I've been scuba diving at depths of 90 feet in spite of a prior perceived concern about drowning; crawled through muddy claustrophobic spaces while spelunking in a cave with a tiny flashlight; and I participated in various contact sports as a youth. For several years I've preached the Word of God on occasion in environments that required a measure of courage. But one of the most risky endeavors has definitely been starting a new business.

Entrepreneurs who launch new businesses often epitomize the risk taker. A man who discovers a treasure and sells everything he owns just to buy the land in which the treasure is buried is a risk-taking entrepreneur. Let us therefore consider this analogy of faith from the business world. Several years ago I was honored to be the invited keynote speaker at a conference on entrepreneurship at the acclaimed Owen School of Business Management at Vanderbilt University in Nashville, Tennessee. I spoke primarily concerning the impact of a company founder's personal philosophy of life on the resulting policies and culture of a company built on those principles. I shared how two of my strongly held values permeated my decision-making processes in both companies, namely *integrity* (i.e., honesty and honoring your obligations) and *altruism* (i.e., serving the needs of others with unselfish good intentions). I then explained to the audience of business leaders that I had frequently perceived a parallel between a life of faith, in the Judeo-Christian sense, and a life of an entrepreneur. As a scientist-entrepreneur of two businesses and as a cofounder of several non-profit organizations thus far, I know the principle of risk taking very well, even as it applies to the secular business world.

Building a successful company from the ground up takes a lot of faith (risk-taking belief in action) in something yet unseen. For every glide path to success there are countless obstacles and mistakes in judgment that can result in failure of a new business opportunity. If not detected and corrected quickly, these problems can result in the closure of the business. Yet, most successful entrepreneurs have a vision and a passion to see their dreams succeed in spite of the risks they face during the roller-coaster ride. The vision is often a new concept that hasn't been fully tested by someone else. I'm not talking about merely purchasing an existing cookie-cutter franchise where everything is turn-key ready or inheriting a 40-year-old successful company from your parents; I'm talking about starting from nothing with only a vision! That is *ex nihilio,* breathing life into a business plan, a written document that outlines some of the founder's vision and financial projections for the future. Then, months and years of follow through in hard work are required. It is extremely rare to experience an ethical overnight success in business.

What I have learned in business and as an advocate for economic development is that the mark of entrepreneurial greatness in the eyes of fellow businessmen and women is measured by the amount of risk that is taken and the tenacity to keep on pressing forward toward the vision in spite of obstacles. Often the vision undergoes metamorphosis to redefine the opportunity and how to best reach the goal of sustainable profitability. Yet, the management of risk is the key ingredient. Risk produces fear, both real and imagined dangers. Fear stifles most of us and stops us in our tracks, often before we've even started. Faith requires facing risk with tenacity. I especially admire entrepreneurs who have been successful at overcoming many obstacles, *and* have done so with integrity and altruism. That is why I named my two companies after these virtues—IntegriDerm and ALtruis. Consider the following exemplary entrepreneurs:

- Walt Disney — innovator of animated films and family entertainment

- Alfred Nobel — inventor of TNT and benefactor of the Nobel Prize foundation

- Thomas Edison and Michael Faraday — serial inventors of electrical and mechanical devices

- Henry Ford — innovator of automotive manufacturing and employment policies

- Marie & Pierre Curie — married scientists who discovered radioactivity

- John D. Rockefeller — aggregator of industries and philanthropist

- Steve Jobs — entrepreneur of leap-frog computer technologies with the Apple Macintosh computer line

- George Washington Carver — horticulture scientist who discovered multiple uses for peanuts to replace the Southern United States' dependence on cotton

- Fred Smith — founder of Federal Express and paradigm shifter for shipping packages overnight

- Alexander Graham Bell — inventor of telegraph and telephone technologies

What did this diverse group of individuals all have in common? They had "visions" or "dreams" of the unseen, and they worked with tenacity to accomplish them. They were not deterred by temporary disappointments and setbacks. They persisted against all odds of success. Their names are commonplace. Had they not worked hard at their "dreams," they would likely be obscured from the history books. "Dreams" and ideas are a dime a dozen, but entrepreneurial success requires hard work! Great ideas without hard work, are just that—great ideas. Great ideas have no impact on society unless they are reduced to practice, as a patent attorney is apt to say, and effectively marketed.

In the secular realm, people often have belief and confidence in themselves (i.e., their education, training, expertise, track record of success, or their network of colleagues). They also trust in investment capital, a fortunate business climate, a new opportunity to serve an unmet market need, the stock market, etc. Nonetheless, they still demonstrate a form of faith (risk-taking belief in action). It is just "secular" faith in something other than the Sovereign God Almighty. How do you think that today's *ethical* entrepreneur-leaders have become successful in business? Mere belief that one will reap unseen rewards is not enough. It takes belief in action to realize the rewards. The founders need to raise the investment capital or loans, hire and retain the staff, effectively utilize legal and accounting expertise, establish manufacturing, marketing, and advertising, etc. After believing in the idea or "vision," then *hard work* is required, and a lot of it. Belief alone is just a "dream" or an idea.

In the Book of James, we learn that faith without works (deeds) is dead.

> *What good is it, my brothers, if a man claims to have faith but has no deeds? ...faith by itself, if it is not accompanied by action, is dead...Show me your faith without deeds, and I will show you my faith by what I do...do you want evidence that faith without deeds is useless?...[Abraham's] faith and his actions were working together, and his faith was made complete by what he did* (James 2:14-22).

Faith without action is not faith...it is merely a belief. God commends his own sons and daughters in His Kingdom to have not only belief in Him and His power, but belief in action. In James, we learn that genuine faith is demonstrated not by what we merely hold as thoughts within our minds, rather by what we do in our actions while trusting Him.

We do reap what we sow. If we sow in faith into the Kingdom, we shall reap from the Kingdom a harvest for His will and purposes. But, if we sow into ourselves (e.g., our agendas, desires, and sin) or we don't work hard, we will not reap from the Kingdom. If you plant the wrong seed, it will give rise to unwelcome weeds. Have you noticed that nowhere in the Bible is a lazy man or woman ever commended? Think about it. God only uses hardworking, purposeful, diligent, tenacious, and busy people to accomplish great things for His Kingdom. He bypasses the lazy (see Heb. 6:12) and doesn't bless them. The movements of God are not established by the hands or minds of lazy men and women. The Book of Proverbs is filled with examples of blessings as the benefits of hard work. Productivity is the result of hard work applied in the proper context with the right tools of the trade.

When I launched my two entrepreneurial companies in the fall of 1998, I had a secure scientist-professor position that was funded by a multi-million dollar endowment in the bank. By the grace of God (see Deut. 8:18), I had been privileged to be among the youngest to receive an endowed chair position in the USA, at the age of only 36. I could have continued in that line of work as an employee in some capacity until retirement, either there or in subsequent similar roles. I was not required to become an entrepreneur.

The challenges I faced in starting the companies carried substantial risks: (1) Although I had launched and managed several non-profit organizations as a volunteer, I had never started a for-profit company; (2) The first of our four children would enter college soon; (3) I had no personal money to invest in the new business opportunities. Money is the fuel that makes the business engine run smoothly. Without it, great ideas are just that—great ideas; (4) Scientific technical companies almost always start with preexisting issued patents, yet none of my own issued patents would be used by the new companies. My companies' intellectual property would be built after launching the firms; (5) I was launching the two companies in Alabama, which was not considered to be the most fruitful environment for scientific entrepreneurs or for obtaining investment capital. Conventional thought would say that the companies should have been started on the East or West coasts of the USA, which had critical mass in biomedical research; (6) I did not want to disappoint my family by giving up financial security as an employee and potentially lose money with a failed business as an entrepreneur; and (7) I didn't want to disappoint my investors, employees, and colleagues interested in seeing our science industry mature in Alabama. In summary, it was all on the line! That is what business risk is all about, just like the man in Matthew chapter 13 who sold all he had to buy a treasure-laden field.

I have been tested in my faith over the years of running my companies. Technology firms are typically dependent on investment capital. I raised some start-up investments during the first year, and was subsequently accountable to those outside investors. Each quarter, they received a progress report including both the advances and difficulties encountered along the journey. They, too, were sharing in the risk-reward relationship along with me as the founder. Both of us had accepted risks—they that their investment might result in a loss of some or all of their money, and me that the company could possibly fail disrupting my career. In that event, I would face the burden of being unemployed and possibilities of facing company and personal debts or a bankruptcy filing.

In order for there to be an "up side" to investments, there must also be a "down side." Investors are not guaranteed that the business plan will be successful. It is frequently a formidable challenge for an entrepreneur to convince the investors that the business plan has minimized possible risks and maximized possibility of success, thus granting an anticipated favorable return-on-investment (ROI). However, the ROI frequently results in a loss. It is reported that Walt Disney approached hundreds of potential lenders or investors before finding a single person or institution that would join in his speculative deal to create animated films. So, it takes faith to be a company founder, and it also takes faith to be an investor, especially in a speculative business endeavor, such as the scientific research and development (R&D) sector. I am quite grateful to have experienced working with a number of high net worth "angel" investors, who had been serial entrepreneurs. Not only did they directly help with their cash investments, but their business insights have often been quite helpful to an entrepreneur. They've walked down similar paths before. So, an entrepreneur can learn from their history of successes and failures in other firms.

We encountered another major obstacle that was very difficult. The years of 2001–2003 were among the most difficult in the history of the biotechnology industry for raising money. It was extremely difficult, with many companies cutting back on staff and expenditures and/or failing. My companies were not immune to those adverse market forces, when a large number of scientific firms ran out of money and failed. To deal with this unfortunate climate, we had to drastically reduce our staff and cut back our expenditures in Draconian fashion. That was very unpleasant for me. In addition to the difficulties in attempting to raise investments, debt financing is quite difficult for R&D companies prior to profitability. We've also experienced that problem firsthand. Fortunately by the hand of God, IntegriDerm was acquired by another complementary pharmaceutical research firm.

One very pragmatic challenge that I have faced is even quite unusual for so-called "Christian" businessmen. God had prompted me in my spirit that any company that I launch should abstain from institutional venture capital (VC) for financing if at all possible, even though VC financing is the typical practice in science and technology companies. In exchange for their VC money being at risk, the managers of VC funds expect extremely high rates of ROI, such as 50-70 percent per annum per investment in my industry. I know many VC managers, and I've heard numbers that high as they are attempting to decide whether they'll do a deal or not. Many of their investments fail, so they are looking only for slam-dunk or "guaranteed" deals with a great upside potential. In addition, they place a lot of legal restrictions on "their" money to attempt to limit their risks within the company they are investing in.

My interactions with numerous high net-worth individuals (and some worth hundreds of millions of dollars) have revealed that two forces drive most of their decisions—*greed* to obtain more wealth during a bullish rising market and *fear* to protect wealth during a declining market. I've also been privileged to discern and see firsthand many times how insidiously strong the god of mammon has control over almost everyone, whether rich or poor, whether Christian or not. Believers, please listen to this warning! We servants of the King of kings should not serve the false god of comfort and the pursuit of wealth. Perhaps that is why the issue of money and possessions is one of the most common themes of the teachings of Jesus.

"CHRISTIAN" BUSINESSMEN ARE RARE

Many of you will probably be surprised at what I'm about to say—I've observed that there are not many genuine "Christian" businessmen and businesswomen. You're either a serious Christian operating within the Kingdom of God or you're are a businessman or businesswoman operating in the world's schematic (see Lk. 16:13). Seldom do I encounter uncompromised Kingdom-focused businessmen and businesswomen. Brothers and sisters, it is a shame and gives a bad testimony to unbelievers when our lives in business look just like everyone else—driven by competitiveness, greed, self-promotion, deception, dishonest gain, and imbalanced priorities. We believers are commanded to not be conformed to the pattern of this world (see Rom. 12:1-2). Fortunately there are some—but I speculate a small number—Kingdom-minded business leaders today. For instance, I have a friend, Dale Cathey, the founder of Craft Brothers construction company and the affiliated Servants of Christ ministry in Birmingham. He and his team of employees strive to do their business and ministry activities in accordance with the revelation of the Kingdom as a "Joseph Company" model. I am grateful to know this brother and his colleagues.

Often so-called Christian businessmen or businesswomen say to themselves, "Oh, I'll just make the money and then someday in the future I'll give it away once I've amassed the wealth." Well, perhaps they might, and then again perhaps something might arise to interfere with those good intentions. There is no better time to get in alignment with the Kingdom than today! If you are a Christian in business, please transition from the kingdom of this world's business practices into the virtuous principles of the Kingdom of God (including honesty, integrity, hard work, generosity, altruism, etc.). The two are mutually incompatible, and only the latter will yield eternal rewards.

The promptings of the Holy Spirit within me concerning investment options are based on an understanding of two things.

First, in Ezekiel chapters 18 and 22, God addresses in the harshest terms that lending money at high interest rates is detestable, and even deserving of death! Now that's strong. He also speaks elsewhere in the Scriptures (e.g., Prov. 28:8) about the dangers of the love of money, the evil of greed, and oppression of the poor. These numerous passages, plus many firsthand reports from scientist-entrepreneur colleagues in this industry about how they were poorly treated at the hands of venture capitalists (often referred to in non-flattering language as "vulture" capitalists) have established a strong warning in my spirit and mind. Therefore, I would have to avoid VC financing of any company that I launch. That has resulted in a self-imposed restriction on the number of viable options that I can pursue for financing. However, I do so out of respect for His Word and the Holy Spirit-led promptings I've received, as I seek to obey. I'd rather spend one day in His courts than a thousand elsewhere. I would rather be led on His narrow path, than be misled by the *ends-justify-the-means* approach that is common in society today.

How about an additional risk that I've experienced in business? ALtruis developed a novel Internet technology, termed the ALtruis Aggregator, based on a patent-pending technology that was revealed to me by God during a time of prayer and fasting. This remarkable technology provides Top-10 search engine rankings online, and drives millions of webpage views annually within the award-winning ALtruis Biomedical Network, which is one of the largest collections of healthcare informational websites online. When the invention was revealed to me, I immediately maxed out four credit cards in order to enable it to work. For several days we received phone calls from the credit cards' anti-fraud detection units asking us whether this was intentional or if our cards had been stolen. (Note that I'm not advocating that anyone max out their credit cards. Fortunately we could eventually service this short-term debt obligation.)

It took real faith on my part, and a hefty measure of trust from my loving wife in support, to see this "dream" become a reality during that year. I knew that it would work extremely well even before we deployed it, as I had the faith to see it while it was yet within the unseen realm. But the expenses that we incurred very quickly were not pleasant. Furthermore, I had to act to develop the invention, the patent applications, purchase the necessary ingredients (e.g., domain name collection), and hire Gayle Christopher to help design the webpages and write informational content to enable the invention to realize its potential. The ALtruis Aggregator did work extremely well and within that year, as I had envisioned. But, had I just believed in the dream, it would not have been realized. I had to believe in something that was unseen and then act on it in risk-taking steps.

Beyond this, ALtruis LLC has an unusual "mission" to provide quality information for free (i.e., altruistically) to millions of people each year. So there was cost in building, deploying, and maintaining this Kingdom-centric "business." But, I've done what I know we were supposed to do. It was Holy Spirit inspired within me before it existed online. We also had some critics questioning its viability. After all, I was building a technology outside of my area of expertise, for I am a molecular and cellular biologist, with no information technology expertise. But, I was correct, and I have no regrets at having developed this exciting technology and network of websites. Millions of people have benefited from it each year.

Besides the tests and risks, I've seen the rewards of risk-taking in my businesses. The benefits have been myriad, including potential increased personal net worth, at least on paper, and learning new skills. I've further developed multitasking capabilities as a manager as I deal with pressures from every direction, like juggling flaming bowling balls. In addition, one experiences increased influence in the community and industry, with an expanded network of people in your address book, and occasionally some gratification at successes on projects (e.g., new inventions).

The element of independence as an entrepreneur is good, but it is overrated on occasion. Being your own boss is a double-edged sword. With the autonomy (i.e., not being subordinate to an employer) comes a high level of responsibility for everything (e.g., personnel, financial, legal, management, products, manufacturing, policies, etc.). It is humorously said that entrepreneurship is the most effective contraceptive. An entrepreneur's life can easily be consumed by all of the urgent issues within the business, if one doesn't manage priorities well.

All that said, it is exciting to breathe a vision into a business plan on paper in "faith" and then witness it become a reality—a company with employees, facilities, and products or services. It takes faith to see into the unseen realm and bring it to pass by subsequent hard work. In a similar vein, if we desire to live a life of genuine faith in the spirit, we must work hard, or else all of the visions and plans will be for nothing. Our actions add meat to the bones of our beliefs. Without actions our beliefs are mere dry bones, good for nothing, even though there is potential within them (see Ezek. 37).

Finally, genuine Christian men and women in business can be effective spiritual leaders of others, and sources of generosity to various ministries. Those in business can seek opportunities to use their influence and self-support to meet the needs of others. God gives business leaders and entrepreneurs various opportunities that are often closed doors to paid pastors in a local church context. If you are in business, take advantage of those distinctions of your calling. God desires to use Kingdom-focused businessmen and women in this critical juncture in history to provide resources and to be door openers for the King of kings. Marketplace ministers have been under-appreciated by the Church's leadership and "members" to date. But, the Kingdom of God is on the move like a lion on a hunt, and He is raising up many Kingdom-centric marketplace ministers in this season.

Chapter Three

QUESTIONS

1. Are you a risk taker or are you risk averse (i.e., seldom seeking new challenges)?

2. How does your own personality, training, and background limit or stimulate your level of trust in God?

3. Have you ever wanted to start a new business or career or ministry?

4. Is God calling you to take steps outside of your comfort zone?

5. Since greater than 95 percent of all Christians are not employed within the local church or other Judeo-Christian ministries, how important is it to "minister" within the "secular" marketplace?

6. If you are not a wealthy individual, imagine that you become wealthy with a high net worth. How would you invest "your" wealth into the Kingdom of God?

7. If you are or become "wealthy" by God's grace, would you be willing to give *80 percent* of your income earned each month for the Kingdom? Or, here's a clever alternative: Would you be willing to give *one percent* of your total net worth (i.e., your estate's total value; not your income, *per se*) each month for the remainder of your life? For instance, if you had a net worth of one million dollars, would you give $10,000 in the first month and continue one percent of the

total incrementally for life? If you were willing to do one percent per month, how about a higher percentage per month? If not, then why not?

8. What is the single greatest risk you have taken for God?

Chapter Four

SURRENDER!

If anyone would come after Me, he must deny himself and take up his cross daily and follow Me. For whoever wants to save his life will lose it, but whoever loses his life for Me will save it (Luke 9:23-24).

...any of you who does not give up everything he has cannot be My disciple (Luke 14:33).

A dirt-covered, sweaty, exhausted soldier in a foxhole eventually resigns to the fact that his position has suffered too many casualties. He cannot continue to fight. Although he is well trained for everything except this apparent failure, in despondence with only a few bullets remaining in one clip, he ties a portion of white cloth to the end of his rifle barrel. He points it up to the sky to be seen clearly by his enemies a short distance away. He has just declared his intentions. One last enemy bullet strikes his rifle and sends a jolting jerk into his hands clenching the shoulder rest of his weapon just below the dirt line of security. Nonetheless, the white cloth is still visible like a sail drifting loosely from a ship's mast. Everything he's been striving for is now lost.

As the enemy's rifle fire lightens and eventually ceases, his heart is beating at triple pace, not knowing whether his enemies will honor the terms of surrender of the Geneva Convention. Will he be shot without question for having resisted so long in his trench that barely protects the top of his helmet? Will he be fed and cared for? Will he be taunted and forced to dig the graves for the enemy's dead using his bare hands? Or, will he be blindfolded and tortured? As he ponders losing all of his previous rights and privileges as an honorable soldier and citizen of his homeland, he correctly whispers out loud to himself, "If I stay here I'm a dead man, and if I go I'm a dead man!" His rights mean almost nothing to his enemies at that time. After all, they are as angry as a hornets' nest at the heartbreaking frustration of watching some of their own men fall from his bullets. He thinks one last time of his beautiful wife and small children playing back home in a distant land, and he pops his torso up out of the foxhole facing the men he's been fighting, not knowing his fate. He has surrendered!

Nothing less than surrender is what Jesus wants from His disciples. Easier said than done. Paul wrote, *"I have been crucified with Christ and I no longer live, but Christ lives in me. The life I live in the body, I live by faith in the Son of God, who loved me and gave Himself for me"* (Gal. 2:20, emphasis added). Unfortunately, the NIV does not translate this phrase well. It should be, *"...I live by faith of the Son of God..."*. There is a substantial difference between faith "in" and faith "of" the Son of God. His faith operating within us is vastly superior to our own feeble attempts. His faith holds inherent power that is imparted to enable us to raise the dead, heal the sick, and move mountains. When Jesus sent out his disciples two-by-two he imparted His faith into them. Otherwise they could not perform spiritual warfare, such as casting out demons and healing the sick, as the Scriptures testify. The disciples just needed to be surrendered "dead men" who were obedient as channels for His superior faith to flow through...that's all.

This truth is further illuminated by, *"Let us fix our eyes on Jesus, the author and perfecter of our faith, who for the joy set before Him endured the cross, scorning the shame, and sat down at the right hand of the throne of God."* (Heb. 12:2, emphasis added). Since it is Jesus' faith within His chosen believers and He is the author writing the script for our faith journey, it has nothing (or very little) to do with "our" faith and essentially everything to do with "His" faith. Just as *His salvation* is imparted to us by His grace, *His faith* is also imparted to us by His grace. Just as His righteousness is imputed to us, His faith is deposited within us. Reliance on our "own" faith will lack true supernatural spiritual power. We just need to tap into His faith!

God doesn't want us to be anything less than fully devoted disciples, willing to surrender our lives for His purposes. A dead man has no rights. A dead man has no privileges. A dead man has no agenda. A dead man has no power in himself. A dead man can have life in this world only if he is "raised from the dead" by the resurrection power of God Almighty. A true disciple is a "dead" man who has been raised to life by the indwelling, filling, and re-filling power of the Holy Spirit. A dead man must continue to live as a dead man toward his own selfish desires.

A dead man empowered with His faith is a sight to behold – the ultimate spiritual oxymoron. It is this release of God's supreme power through surrendered human conduits that causes the enemy to shutter in fear. The accuser of the brethren is helpless to stop the power of God Almighty flowing through a surrendered servant. Yes my friends, the enemy is actually afraid of us when we're operating in Jesus' faith. God's power flows through us as His servants once our natural power steps aside. A dead man or woman empowered by His faith is a mighty warrior in the Kingdom of God!

Jesus told us that we would perform greater works than those He performed. *"I tell you the truth, anyone who has faith in me will do what I have been doing. He will do even greater things than these, because I am going to the Father"* (Jn. 14:12). His faith operating within the multitude of His disciples around the globe can have miraculous impact around the world at any moment. The indwelling, filling, and re-filling of the Holy Spirit (subsequent to Jesus' departure from the Earth) enables the greater works both individually and through the plurality of His surrendered disciples.

Recently during ministry I humorously coined the phrase the "Charcoal Club" to describe what we believers are, once we've finally surrendered as disciples. Charcoal is produced by placing wood in a fire to burn off the volatile oils, waxes, and most of the combustible materials. However, once charcoal has been produced it can be placed inside of an even hotter smelting oven to melt metals, such as iron. The first burn to produce charcoal from wood resembles the surrender of our own natural power with all of its limitations. This first burn is the believer-to-disciple transformation. The second burn consumes even the charcoal itself and represents the power of God operating within us as surrendered servants. His power is massively more effective than our own talents and abilities. He can use us once we're just a lump of coal! His power is released when we are yielded and obedient. As members of the Charcoal Club, we're not good for much of anything, and we're not highly esteemed by the world. But, we can be consumed for His higher calling, as He reveals His power through us.

There is a very funny scene in the movie *Monty Python and the Holy Grail.* A medieval knight in black armor protects a small bridge over a worthless little stream that anyone could simply bypass a few feet downstream. As the knight blocks the route, he looks frightening in stature and declares to all whom he encounters this phrase, *"None shall pass!"* Then, during a battle with King Arthur, all of the black knight's limbs are chopped off, one by one. As he sequentially loses body parts, he says ridiculous things as the scene progresses, *"...Tis but a scratch...Oh, had enough, eh?...Just a flesh wound...I'm invincible...."* In spite of numerous mortal wounds, the black knight refuses to surrender his futile position and die. He looks so absurd boasting and trying to fight without limbs or weapons.

The black knight reminds me of many of us believers who lack spiritual power, because we're relying on the wrong thing. We look so silly when we try to live in the strength of our own flesh (e.g., knowledge, understanding, talents, beauty, and agendas), without His power operating through the indwelling Holy Spirit. We need to know how to die to self. We need to submit and let Him thrive within us and be victorious through us. We can live a fully effective spiritual life only if we are dead to ourselves and made alive to His will and His Kingdom.

In a revelatory dream concerning this death-transformation process, God demonstrated to me the process of being tied down on an operating table, as a surgeon with a huge knife painfully carved away flesh. The dream ended with a picture of a half man/half machine with a giant multi-ton steel axle, like those used by a locomotive or a semi truck. The axle had replaced the natural legs. The process of going from natural soul-ish power to supernatural power was clearly demonstrated. Our triune beings need not only the indwelling Holy Spirit within our *spirit* compartment, but our two other compartments, the *soul* (i.e., mind and emotions) and physical *body*, need to be progressively governed by the Holy Spirit as well. In some cases the forces of unholy demonic influence need to be removed from these latter two compartments. Spiritual maturation results from obediently sweeping out the dust of corruption from the other two compartments of our lives.

The first-century apostle Paul wrote, *"For to me, to live is Christ and to die is gain"* (Phil. 1:21). Even in physical death, disciples of Jesus have nothing to lose and everything to gain. We're admonished to live *"not by* [our] *might, nor by* [our] *power, but by My Spirit"* says the Lord (Zech. 4:6, emphasis added). I urge you, go ask a mature devoted disciple of Jesus if he or she regrets having received the precious gift of salvation in Jesus and the benefits of a yielded servant's life? They undoubtedly wouldn't trade those experiences, sufferings, and benefits for anything, and they have yet to experience the overwhelming and inexpressible glory and joy of Heaven. The best is yet to come. Faith says that Heaven is more real than the physical realities we experience each day.

In the Fall of 1997, David Barber, the District Attorney of Birmingham, invited my son Isaac and me to attend my second Promise Keepers meeting, which was held at Legion Field in Birmingham. As Wellington Boone preached about the need for men to surrender to the will of the Father God, I was moved to tears by the Holy Spirit's touch. I realized that I had been operating at a 95 percent level in my Christian experience for many years, holding back an extra five percent that I wanted to retain control of in my life. The five percent issues weren't even areas of obvious sin. They were issues that many would consider as good things, such as career plans. God wants all of us, not 95 percent. He is Adonai, the Lord (the Boss) of both Heaven and Earth. The Lord wants to be in control of our lives. Are we willing to surrender to Him?

As we mature from being a believer into being a disciple, we transition from decisions of "right vs. wrong" to decisions about "excellent vs. good." As former patterns of sin become memories of the distant past, we grow in discernment at new levels and become increasingly sensitive to "new" areas of sin, which would not have been on our radar screen previously. The final five percent (or 25 percent for that matter) that needs to be surrendered can even be within the realm of "excellent vs. good" choices. The final five per-cent doesn't even need to be overt sin. But, God wants 100 percent surrender. He can work best with those who are genuine servants, who don't claim to have any rights of their own. A servant has no right to say, "No, I won't do that." Our faith engine starts firing on all eight cylinders when we're at the place of 100 percent surrender. I distinctly remember sensing the Lord saying to me in January 2000, that if we don't exhibit 100-percent trust then it isn't really faith. He doesn't want the 95 percent. He wants full trust.

I had been a serious evangelical believer and had ministered for the past two decades in various capacities, yet that day's simple mes-sage came to me in the power of the Holy Spirit and touched me deeply. I left my seat in the stands and went down on the football field in the rain, and in tears I declared to God that He could have control of everything in my life—my family, career, the future business I was planning, ministry, etc. I surrendered! I wouldn't trade all of my prior life until that time for the season of maturation and blessings I've received since then. My son Isaac was also moved greatly that day, and God has blessed him with a great anointing for prayer, innovation, and creativity as he has grown in obedience to the Almighty.

It is usually a stretch of our minds to live in the faith realm. Our minds will hold us back if we don't volitionally take our thoughts cap-tive. We have some areas in our lives where it is easy to have faith and other areas where it is difficult to have faith. It seems like we have dif-ferent compartments in our minds. Yet, from God's perspective, no one area is inherently more difficult than another. After all, El Shaddai, our all-sufficient God, can accomplish anything effortlessly. For some of us it seems difficult or impossible for God to do certain tasks, such as to instantaneously heal someone or raise someone from the dead, but for other individuals who have faith in that area the issue is quite simple. Our minds must be engaged to agree with the indwelling Holy Spirit, who desires for a fuller manifestation of faith in all areas of our lives.

We need to grow in the fear of the Lord and trust Him when a challenge or circumstance doesn't make sense. We need to choose to stand at the end of the diving board by the tips of our toes. Faith won't happen while you're sitting on the poolside looking up the ladder at the diving board perched high overhead. Sitting on the poolside will produce an emotion, perhaps fear or anticipation or excitement. But, faith commences when you ascend the ladder and position your toes on the edge of the board. Then, with your heart racing, you accept the risk knowing that you are about to experience something that you do not control. That is faith!

MY EARLY DAYS IN THE FAITH JOURNEY

Until I was 18 years old, I was a church-attending, religious, young man with many career and personal aspirations. I was a "dreamer" and envisioned from the age of seven that I would be a scientist-doctor working with microscopes. I was a passionate, expressive dancer. My dear sister, Theresa, jokes that I "invented" *break dancing* during the Disco era, and well before its time of acceptance. I really loved to dance, even to this day. I came from a hardworking family with a good reputation in our farming community in northeastern Kansas. However, I don't believe that I had yet fully understood that salvation from our sins is the result of *grace alone,* although I had probably been exposed to that truth via occasional Youth for Christ meetings and the attempts of a godly Christian man, Clarence Todd, my science teacher in high school. Like most of my family and friends who were regular church attenders, I thought that we were supposed to do good deeds in order to obtain an entrance into Heaven. Incorrectly I assumed as I had been taught that our admission into Heaven was based upon what *we* did, as opposed to what *He* did.

However, in 1977 while attending the University of Kansas, I became aware for the first time from reading the Bible that salvation is by grace (unmerited favor) alone (see Eph. 2:8-9). I became a genuine believer, although it is formally possible that I was a genuine believer at some earlier date, yet without fully comprehending in my mind what might have already happened in my spirit. As an evidence of that decision, I was re-baptized as an adult in the university swimming pool as a public declaration, while attending a campus-based evangelical church, New Life.

Shortly after the decision to accept Jesus' free gift of salvation, I experienced firsthand some very tough lessons and a good measure of the cost of following. My favorite Bible passage in those early testing

71

times was spoken by Jesus, "...*no one who has left home or brothers or sisters or mother or father or children or fields for Me and the gospel will fail to receive a hundred times as much in the present age (homes, brothers, sisters, mothers, children, and fields—and with them, persecutions) and in the age to come, eternal life*" (Mk. 10:29-30). My extended family had a difficult time understanding what was happening as I attempted to obey the promptings of the Holy Spirit, as best I could understand them as a young believer who was beginning to grow into a disciple. I didn't get everything precisely right, but I was striving to be pleasing to Him. God was clearly calling me to be courageous, obedient, and to move away from the only Christian denomination and religious traditions that my extended family had experienced for generations. As a consequence my parents and siblings likely experienced some puzzling thoughts at my actions. I didn't do this to hurt any of them. I was just striving to follow Jesus and to surrender to His plans for my life in obedience to what I was learning (in most cases for the very first time) from His written Word. However, if we let our fear of our family and friends block us from obedience to God's promptings, we are in sin. Too many believers are held back from obedience to the Lord because of the fear of man.

I know what it means when Jesus said, "*No one who puts his hand to the plow and looks back is fit for service in the kingdom of God*" (Lk. 9:62). Even though my family likely experienced some unpleasant moments dealing with my decisions, I faced more difficulties than them concerning the consequences of these actions in obedience to the Lord. The cost was greater for me. Surrendering to Jesus to become a disciple over the coming months and years ahead cost me relationships with family, friends, classmates at college, and even a girlfriend from high school. Those were tough decisions. I just had to be obedient and walk into the grace of Jesus' arms by faith in expectancy that He would reward those who earnestly seek Him (see Heb. 11:6). As I walked toward Jesus, I had to repent and walk away from many areas of sin patterns that were revealed to me by His logos Word, and be cleansed by the blood of the Lamb. Obedience to God is not easy; at least it wasn't in the earliest stages of sanctification (i.e., being set apart for God) for me. It was a struggle. As we mature, obedience becomes increasingly easier and sin less enticing. As we walk the journey of righteousness, the "highway of the Lord" before us narrows into a footpath. As we grow in awareness of His will, our former liberties and relationships to people should be surrendered as we advance onto the increasingly narrow path of holiness.

I was helped on this initial discipleship journey by two pastors at New Life, Dan Goering and Van Birrer, who later officiated at my marriage to Laura. I am grateful for their sacrifice and investment into my early spiritual life while at the University of Kansas, a place known for secular intellectuals and anti-Christian views. Lawrence, Kansas was not a place where one would expect to encounter evangelical believers and to get saved by Jesus. I commend all of the soldiers of Christ who keep evangelizing and discipling on hard soil in our universities. Those valiant soldiers deserve honor, because they are on the frontlines of reclaiming lost territory for the King. They do so in the face of opposition by the spiritual forces of darkness behind the college's faculty and administrators, who are set on conforming the students to worldly standards and deceptive philosophies.

Another pastor gifted in teaching at New Life, Paul Abbott, once preached a message that has not been easily forgotten. He said that a transformed life is what God desires to use in the world today. Transformation requires surrender. Transformation means that the old is replaced by the new. Let us not deceive ourselves into thinking that we are fully transformed and yielded, if in fact we are not. Are we holding back five percent or 25 percent for our own control, where we refuse to let His will prevail? Do you ever have a hard time with your conscience when you are required to say, pray, or sing the phrase, "Jesus is Lord"? For the first two decades of my Judeo-Christian walk, I had various times where I just couldn't say it in all honesty...and I didn't want to be hypocritical because I knew I was holding back in one or more areas of my life. Jesus said, *"Whoever has My commands and obeys them, he is the one who loves Me. He who loves Me will be loved by My Father, and I too will love him and show Myself to him"* (Jn. 14:21). The key is in loving Jesus by obeying His words. Therefore, without obedience there can be no real love.

THE COST OF BEING A SURRENDERED DISCIPLE

Many people find that it is easy to accept Jesus as Savior and to receive forgiveness of his or her sins. There's no down side to that proposition. But, it is much harder to accept Him as Lord (boss) of your life, as we expect that He might mess with some of the things that we like to do or to control. Jesus wants us to be yielded *disciples*, not just so-called "Christians" or *believers* with presumed fire insurance policies. I even ponder whether presumed fire insurance policies alone are very effective on the Day of Judgment (see Jas. 2:14-26) for some individuals. We need to pursue righteousness, holiness, and perform good deeds in our daily lives as surrendered overcoming disciples. Will your name be preserved for all eternity in the Lamb's Book of Life in the heavenlies? Paul wrote, *"I pray also that the eyes of your heart may be enlightened in order that you may know the hope to which He has called you, the riches of His glorious inheritance in the saints, and His incomparably great power for us who believe"* (Eph. 1:18-19a). We must glance into our eternal future for perspective (see Lk. 16:19-31).

Faith is not easy or comfortable. If your life is easy and comfortable, examine your inner thoughts and outward actions. Are you demonstrating any risk-taking actions? Are you genuinely surrendered to God's will and leading in your life? Some of us operate with a penny's worth of faith, and some of us with a dime's worth, and some of us with one hundred dollar's worth. It is not productive to just envy others who seem to have large amounts of faith and marvel in their testimonies. You must start the faith journey somewhere. If you currently use a dime's worth of faith, then build upon it consistently and then you'll soon have a quarter's worth. It is a life of progressing from faith victory on to other faith victories. Although we all experience some disappointments and delays along the journey, there's no point at which it is acceptable to get off the faith treadmill and rest or retire. No matter how old, or what condition our bodies are in, there's no acceptable time to quit living a surrendered life of faith. And, it sure is a lot of fun to surf the crest of a faith wave. Been there, done that many times!

One of the hardest things for most of us to surrender is our *pride*. We build our self-confidence around our prior successes, accomplishments, capabilities and skills, and in some instances our relationships to others (e.g., pedigree, family, or social clubs and organizations). Confidence and self-assurance are good virtues when coupled with humility. But, confidence can also drive us into arrogance, self-seeking independence of the living God, and even rebellion. I am very fond of the poem entitled "Ozymandias" by Percy B. Shelley (1792-1822), in which he describes the boastful inscription on a stone monument attributed to the Egyptian Pharaoh Rameses II:

I met a traveler from an antique land
Who said: Two vast and trunkless legs of stone
Stand in the desert. Near them, on the sand,
Half sunk, a shattered visage lies, whose frown,
And wrinkled lip, and sneer of cold command,
Tell that its sculptor well those passions read,
Which yet survive, stamped on these lifeless things,
The hand that mocked them, and the heart that fed,
And on the pedestal these words appear:
"My name is Ozymandias, King of Kings:
Look upon my works, ye Mighty, and despair!"
Nothing beside remains. Round the decay
Of that colossal wreck, boundless and bare
The lone and level sands stretch far away.

God is opposed to the proud, but gives grace to the humble. In my own life, one of the single greatest spiritual struggles has been between my own pride and obedience to the humbling acts and ways of the Holy Spirit. In large part that has been due to the fact that God has greatly blessed and anointed me with many talents, giftings, accomplishments, achievements, and skills. Since I am an effective communicator verbally and in written form, I've had the tendency to be boastful for much of my life.

Pride and humility are in opposition to one another. The pride of our "natural" inner man or woman cries out for self-seeking comfort, for recognition by others, and to be in control. The "I, me, and my" centrism must be crucified daily (see Gal. 2:20). That is an area where I've personally struggled during the process of maturation. May we learn this lesson of surrender in this world before it is too late. Our pride is one of the greatest obstacles to salvation and beyond that to living a Holy Spirit-filled and sanctified life of power. Once we surrender our pride, the Holy Spirit can lead us into all truth. If our pride is not surrendered in this life, then regrettably we'll take it with us into a godless eternity.

Two sidebar comments related to this topic that I've observed about successful leaders are: (1) Success draws to oneself false friends and real enemies; and (2) If you desire to be a leader in front, don't be surprised if people talk behind your back. Leaders take a lot of public and private criticism. It takes a stiff spine to stand up as a leader and fight against the fear of man. It also takes balance in our spiritual lives to have courage and confidence, yet without developing a critical judgmental spirit and pride that we've achieved things in our own strength. Leaders must protect against taking offenses, of which there will be plenty of opportunities, and converting them into a bitter unforgiving spirit.

God has been instructing me by watching my children. My second daughter, Jeannette, is a beautiful example of a highly talented and gifted individual. She is loving and considerate and doesn't let her accomplishment in music or academics produce pride. My oldest son, Isaac, likewise has done exceptionally well academically, yet he doesn't boast of his accomplishments. They are two examples instructing me in how I can improve my character. This is an area where my wife and children are leading me by example. I am so glad to have them in my life. Furthermore, if it weren't for the gracious support of my loving wife, I would not be available for ministry trips around the globe. Without Laura's understanding and selflessness, the influence granted to our family would be more limited. As a result Path Clearer ministries' goals and accomplishments would be diminished.

In Deuteronomy chapter 5, Moses speaks of the consequences of disobedience versus obedience to God's commandments. Although the effects of a father's sin are visited up to the third and fourth generations, the effects of a father's righteous obedience is love from the heavenly Father up to a thousand generations. That could represent ca. 20,000 years, which is figurative of an eternal blessing. The effects of sin have a statute of limitations on Earth, whereas the effects of a righteous life of love and obedience to the Lord last for eternity! This is certainly great news. Our submitted and obedient lives produce eternal blessings. May we yield to the counsel of the Holy Spirit and surrender!

Chapter Four

QUESTIONS

1. Do you know Jesus as Savior and Lord? If not, why not? Are you in a relationship with Him?

2. Since our greatest strengths can also be our greatest weaknesses, list several of your personal strengths or capabilities. Then, list possible ways in which the devil might pervert these good attributes for his evil intentions.

3. Have you repented for clinging onto your life, your family, your career, your education, etc. without surrendering these things to Jesus?

4. Are you pushing Jesus away from you in specific areas of your life and not allowing Him to be Lord (boss) of those areas?

5. A failure to surrender can result from many causes, such as fear, pride, independence, selfishness, pleasure, comfort, etc. List the issues that are holding you back from trusting God more.

6. Which major circumstances from your childhood contribute to your willingness to surrender to God today?

7. Explain the difference between being in a relationship with Jesus and being a religious "Christian."

8. Why are there so few genuine *disciples* among the many *believers*? What is wrong with this?

Chapter Five

FARMING: SEED AND HARVEST

Do not be deceived: God cannot be mocked. A man reaps what he sows. The one who sows to please his sinful nature, from that nature will reap destruction; the one who sows to please the Spirit, from the Spirit will reap eternal life. Let us not become weary in doing good, for at the proper time we will reap a harvest if we do not give up (Galatians 6:7-9).

Practical lessons of faith are easily learned on a farm. My extended family lives in Good Intent, a small rural community northwest of Atchison, Kansas. Good Intent consists mostly of German and Irish Catholic farmers, who help one another in times of serious personal difficulty. On occasion when a farmer is injured or is too ill to work, the community rallies together, and they will plant or harvest the crops for his family. The neighbors provide their own tractors, equipment, and time at no cost. I've seen this remarkable sign of altruism several times in our home community. It is a demonstration of unselfish love in action. On multiple occasions up to a dozen tractors have rolled into a field and then finished the entire job in one or two days. At lunch or dinner, the farmers' wives prepare food and everyone will share together in a spirit of cooperation that goes beyond petty annoyances with one's neighbors. The dusty, sweaty men will often end the evening sharing a meal or chilled beer together while swapping stories. And on top of this, the community typically meets the needs of the family in distress before they attend to their own fields.

This remarkable occurrence is well worth witnessing, as it is so encouraging. Some skeptical city-dwellers might doubt that this type of altruism still happens today in America's heartland, just as it did in the 19th century. However, I assure you that the community of Good Intent is a real place and these families are real! I lived there. It reminds me of what a prototypical German-American Amish community might do at times. I have the privilege of knowing an Amish friend who believes in a miracle-working God. Elvie Miller and his brother run a family business, Meadowlark Log Homes, in Libby, Montana. The Amish are known for pooling resources and labor for the benefit of the whole community.

We sometimes overlook the fact that farms really are *businesses* that produce products. It takes a lot of hard work to run an effective and profitable farm. This is especially true in today's economy. In the USA today the prices of grains and livestock have not risen in over three decades, yet there has been substantial inflation in the cost of living. Tractors cost much more, fuel costs much more, and building supplies cost much more. Farms are barely surviving. Many farmers feel as if they are draining the figurative last drop of blood out of a turnip. Efficiency and higher yields have sustained just enough profit to keep family farms viable. And the successor generations can't afford to run the farms and make the interest payments on the land or implement purchases.

I find that farmers understand well the concept of faith, and often better than those who work a job as employees. Years ago I had a conversation with one of my non-farmer relatives, who worked a job in the city. I remember him saying to me, "Your dad is a farmer. Therefore, he *must* trust in God to provide. But, I'm better at providing for my needs than God is." Although I don't agree with his latter perspective on Jehovah Jireh's provision (see Deut. 8:18), I do agree that farmers experience a form of "faith" during each yearly cycle. Farmers plant seeds without knowing whether rains will arrive at the right times and in sufficient quantity to grow their crops. The farmers don't control the rain cycles. They invest money, time, and energy in planting, hoping for a good harvest. In addition, experienced farmers know the low odds of an outstanding "bumper crop," when the harvest exceeds the anticipated or normal level. They've experienced droughts, floods, infestations of pests and weeds, and wind damage to their crops. *"Land that drinks in the rain often falling on it and that produces a crop useful to those for whom it is farmed receives the blessing of God. But land that produces thorns and thistles is worthless and is in danger of being cursed. In the end it will be burned"* (Heb. 6:7-8). And, when they have an excellent harvest, they often encounter that the market prices are deflated. So, in spite of an abundant harvest that year, they don't make much more even in the best of times. It takes faith and persistence to continue to plant each year, knowing that your family's financial needs might not be met at harvest time.

Most farmers and all ranchers maintain some livestock, such as cattle. They experience both good and bad years with their herds and the market conditions, which are outside of their control. The herds can run out of hay, feed, a convenient water supply, or face a devastating disease. I sure admire farmers and ranchers, like my father and my relatives in Good Intent for their practical faith! Unlike the landowners of ancient Roman territories, who were held in the highest regard by everyone in society, the landowners of today's American farms are not held in such high esteem. Many are even looked down upon. As much as it depends upon me, I'd like to see them receive their due credit.

As an example of relevance to our walk of faith, let's consider a lesson learned from a feature of a farm tractor. While a boy on the farm, I often drove our red International Harvester tractors to plow, disk, cultivate, or haul various loads. If you have never driven a farm tractor, you may not know that one thing quite distinctive from other motor vehicles is the way in which you assist the steering on a tractor, using one of two rear wheel brakes—one for the left rear tire and one for the right rear tire. On many occasions, the top of the soil in a field may have a crust that appears dry, but only a few inches underneath it can be perilously soft mud. A tractor driver can very quickly go from seemingly safe soil to dangerous sinking soil in a couple of seconds. Very rapid action is required to prevent the tractor from becoming stuck in the mud immediately beneath the veneer of dry soil.

With many hours of experience using the braking-steering system, a well-trained tractor operator can drive through soft mud that would quickly sink an inexperienced driver. The reason is that the wheel with the greatest ease of travel will accelerate faster than the one experiencing the greatest torque of resistance. If you drive through a muddy area, one wheel will spin disproportionately and rapidly sink that side of the tractor up to several feet in depth. But, by carefully using the brake on that side, you can transfer more torque to the other wheel and let the wheel on more solid ground push the entire tractor forward. It takes experience to learn this lesson of applying the appropriate braking pressures.

So, why is this example relevant to our Christian experience? Inexperienced or immature believers often journey dangerously close to the encrusted mud of life. Some even choose to remain associated with the sin influencers of their former non-Christian lives. They plow forward without perceiving the threatening conditions in the path ahead. They haven't developed the ability to discern dangers in advance or to listen carefully to God's rhema revelation about what lies ahead of them. They rapidly sink into the mud and stop their progress. But, mature believers know how to apply the brakes when they encounter the soft ground and effectively manage the situation, so that they don't succumb to sin. Both the immature and the mature will encounter the dry crust-covered schemes of the enemy, but only one of them will drive through it effectively. The mature know how to overcome these obstacles.

Consider another farming analogy. If we sow good seed, then we shall reap a good harvest. If we sow bad seed, then the outcome is already assured long before it comes to pass. In the realm of farming, sowing requires entrusting our seed into God's hands while the seeds are concealed in the soil, for He alone can cause the seeds to germinate and grow. We do our small part by planting the seed, which is analogous to the "death" of the seed, to ensure a future harvest. It takes "faith" to plant seeds, because they disappear and "die" before our very eyes. After the seeds are planted, it takes a long time before the harvest. Yet, we plant with the anticipation of a harvest reward.

Conversely, if we hoard or consume all that we currently have and lack genuine faith to invest or sow our seed for tomorrow's crop, then we will not reap at the anticipated time of harvest (see Prov. 21:20). We are taught, *"From everyone who has been given much, much will be demanded; and from the one who has been entrusted with much, much more will be asked"* (Lk. 12:48b). If we don't invest what we are currently holding in our hands, then that which we have at present will dwindle and pass away. You must continue to, *"Cast your bread upon the waters, for after many days you will find it again"* (Eccl. 11:1). If a farmer eats all of his grain and doesn't save a remnant to plant, then he is very foolish and shortsighted. A portion of grain is needed for the next year's crop (except for hybrid grains, where you must repurchase seed each season).

Jesus taught the parable of the sower:

Others, like seed sown on rocky places, hear the word and at once receive it with joy. But since they have no root, they last only a short time. When trouble or persecution comes because of the word, they quickly fall away. Still others, like seed sown among thorns, hear the word; but the worries of this life, the deceitfulness of wealth and the desires for other things come in and choke the word, making it unfruitful. Others, like seed sown on good soil, hear the word, accept it, and produce a crop—thirty, sixty or even a hundred times what was sown (Mark 4:16-20).

Jesus clearly understood the principles of farming. This parable has at least two alternative spiritual meanings. It usually is interpreted to refer to *different individuals* and their responses to the Word of God that is sown. The conditions of the soil refer to different types of individuals. In the second case, it can alternatively refer to *different parts or seasons of one's life* and the responses at those times to the sown Word. In the latter case, at different times in our Christian lives we receive and germinate the Word to varying degrees of fruitfulness. Regardless of which interpretation applies, the key is to become spiritually productive and generate 30, 60, or 100-fold fruit from what God has invested in us.

SATAN SOWS "WEEDS" IN THE CHURCH

Crop productivity is affected not only by the seed and the soil conditions, but also by interfering weeds. In the Gospel of Matthew,

*Jesus told them another parable: "The kingdom of heaven is like a man who sowed good seed in his field. But while everyone was sleeping, his **enemy** came and sowed weeds among the wheat, and went away. When the wheat sprouted and formed heads, then the weeds also appeared. The owner's servants came to him and said, 'Sir, didn't you sow good seed in your field? Where then did the weeds come from?''An **enemy** did this,' he replied. The servants asked him, 'Do you want us to go and pull them up?''No,' he answered, 'because while you are pulling the weeds, you may root up the wheat with them. Let both grow together until the harvest. At that time I will tell the harvesters: First collect the weeds and tie them in bundles to be burned; then gather the wheat and bring it into my barn' "* (Matthew 13:24-30, emphasis added).

In this parable we learn that the enemy, the devil, is working to prevent a good harvest in the Kingdom of God. Satan uses many strategies to prevent God's destiny from being realized within us, such as an unreceptive hardened heart, troubles, persecution, worries, deceitfulness of wealth, desires for "other" things (e.g., comforts, intelligence, influence, sex, etc.), and putting counterfeits and deceptions around us (e.g., counterfeit "Christians"). Therefore, we need to be good spiritual farmers and know well the condition of our soil and the schemes of our enemy.

Another lesson learned on the farm is that weeds arise in fields naturally. Weeds are an expression of entropy, a physics term meaning that things run downhill toward chaos and disorder. You don't have to plant weeds; they just arise spontaneously from the seeds of prior seasons. The spiritual metaphor used by Jesus serves to warn us on at least two different levels. Problems and conflicts are inevitable in our lives. And, problem individuals will arise to confront us and our appointed destinies, attempting to steal nutrients and water from around us. Jesus said, *"Each day has enough trouble of its own"* (Mt. 6:34b), and *"I have told you these things, so that in Me you may have peace. In this world you shall have trouble. But take heart! I have overcome the world"* (Jn. 16:33). Isn't it encouraging to know that Jesus was tempted in all things on Earth, and yet He overcame those tests? We have a God who can sympathize with our weakness and testings. Because He was an overcomer, He is qualified to grant His authority to us to partner in victories with Him. We shall certainly encounter trials and tribulations—the weeds of life.

Many of the trials and tribulations are put in front of us by the devil. However, they are placed before us with the foreknowledge of the sovereign Lord. The devil has limited authority as a defeated toothless lion. Jesus, the Lion of Judah, can overrule him at any time with His unlimited power and knowledge, for He said, *"All authority in heaven and on earth has been given to Me"* (Mt. 28:18b).

Often people assign an inappropriate level of importance and power to the devil. Many folks don't believe that the devil is real. They are deceived, because he is real. The father of lies and deception has done an effective trick on them. Just as the Scriptures inform us that he who says there is no God is a fool (see Ps. 14:1), so it is also true of those who say that there is no devil. Conversely, many folks give the devil too much credit, as if his power is equivalent to God's in a wrestling match. The devil is not all-knowing, he is not ever-present, he is not eternal; he was created and has limited power (albeit a considerable amount). Many folks incorrectly think that the devil has a half-full glass of power and access. He doesn't. The level of his power and influence can't be quantified, but in the half-full, half-empty glass analogy, God Almighty sure is the winner by an overwhelming margin!

To further illuminate this disparity, consider this hypothetical scenario: Even if God Almighty disappeared, and the four living creatures and the 24 elders surrounding the throne disappeared, and all of the spirits of deceased believers in Heaven including all of our heroes of the Bible disappeared, the devil and his horde of countless demons would be outnumbered two-to-one by the angelic hosts of Heaven! Just think about it, satan is very limited. He wants all of us to be deceived into denying or discounting that he actually exists, or that we fear him because he is more powerful than he actually is. He's just a weed sower and a deceiver! He's the father of lies. The weed sower comes only to steal, kill, and destroy. But, Jesus comes to give us abundant life!

The goal of farming is to provide for your family's needs either directly from the fruits of your labors (e.g., grains, vegetables, meat, etc.) or by selling your goods in the marketplace. The fruits of our labors of faith should be a deep well of provision and prosperity for our own families. As we live by faith and honor His written logos Word, He will uphold us and provide for all of our needs. *"Do not let this Book of the Law* [Torah] *depart from your mouth; meditate on it day and night, so that you may be careful to do everything written in it. Then you will be prosperous and successful"* (Josh. 1:8). As His Word is planted into us, and we obey it with faith, we shall produce a good harvest in due season.

Chapter Five

QUESTIONS

1. Since we shall reap what we sow, what are you sowing into the Kingdom of God?

2. Is it possible that current difficulties in our lives are the consequences of our past bad seeds and/or bad seeds sown by our parents and ancestors?

3. Farmers and gardeners exhibit faith each time they labor preparing the soil and investing in seeds for planting. What aspects of your faith and prayers involve laboring and investing?

4. Have you developed a regular pattern of investing your resources (time, money, spiritual giftings, and passion) into the Kingdom of God? If so, describe the disciplines you have adopted and practiced.

5. Is it difficult for you to generously sow into the needs of widows, orphans, the fatherless, foreigners, and the homeless? What do you expect in return?

6. How does your attitude concerning your uses of "your" money reflect on your faith?

7. How does the busyness of your life distract you from the simplicity of "what is really important"? Are you sowing into what is really important?

Part II

✦

Understanding Prayer

Chapter 6

POWER THROUGH
PASSIONATE PRAYER

During the days of Jesus' life on earth, He offered up prayers and petitions **with loud cries and tears** *to the one who could save Him from death, and He was heard because of His reverent submission. Although He was a son, He learned obedience from what He suffered and, once made perfect, He became the source of eternal salvation for all who obey Him* (Hebrews 5:7-9, emphasis added).

We often encounter young believers who are zealous for things of the Lord. By young, we mean recent "repenters" (as they are referred to in Romania), who have established relationships to Jesus as their Savior within months or a couple of years. They seem to thrive at the newness of the grandeur of the spiritual life that they've just walked into. But often, over time, the passion seems to fade away as the relationship begins to become a religion with a system instead of a living Savior. How do we stay at the top of our spiritual game? Continuing our faith journey with enthusiasm and joy is dependent on two ingredients—passionate prayer and power.

Let's be pragmatic concerning prayer. What works and what does not work? There are many factors impacting whether prayers are answered, such as the specifics of the request, timing, level of passion, persistence, our need versus our want, trust and faith, His will versus our will, worship, effects of spiritual warfare, being tested and disciplined for our own good, and who is asking Him.

We've likely heard the standard line on prayer, "God always answers our prayers. His answers are 'yes,'' no,' or 'later.' " But, there is another biblical answer, "I never heard you. I refuse to even listen to you!" Do you realize that there are numerous Scriptures saying that God refuses to listen to the prayers of stubborn, obstinate, and rebellious sinners? For explicit examples please read: Isaiah 58, Jeremiah 7, Ezekiel 8:18, Zechariah 7:11-13, Psalm 66:18, Proverbs 28:9. I have never heard anyone even mention this topic. So, I started speaking about this principle. Perhaps we just don't always want the *whole counsel* of the Lord. It was a new insight to me in the 1990's. God says that He chooses to not listen to rebellious individuals and groups of individuals who have stuffed cotton in their ears concerning what God is declaring to them. That's hard to make more palatable. God is sovereign and He determines who He wants to listen to.

God wants us to be dependent upon Him to grow and have increased understanding of who He is and how He works. It is said in the Torah that God made His *acts* (actions) known to the people of Israel, but His *ways* (His desires, plans, and means) to Moses, as the two of them were in an intimate relationship as friends. Moses knew how to pray because he enjoyed a deep and close relationship to his Creator (see Deut. 34:10-12). The Bible can be read just like any other book, like a novel or a history book. But, in order to have Holy Spirit-inspired revelation, we must be in relationship with the indwelling Holy Spirit. Some people refer to this as being "filled with the Spirit." In the Book of Acts (and in the Old Testament) we see that the process of being filled happens repeatedly over time. First, at salvation we are indwelt by the promised Holy Spirit, and then (typically later) filled with the Spirit, and then even later refilled with the Spirit, like waves of the sea splashing over us. It seems that we are like leaky buckets that need to be refilled over and over for His purposes. Prayer is one of the means of developing a bilateral relationship with God in which the Holy Spirit guides our thoughts and the words that we voice. The filling and refilling progression involves us being in an intimate relationship of trust, obedience, holiness, and righteousness. The Holy Spirit is eager to participate with us, but we are prone to grieving the sensitive Holy Spirit as we operate in soul-ish self-interest. In addition, note that in some Scriptures the filling process is associated with the *laying on of hands* by those who have journeyed ahead of us in faith with the Spirit. Impartation of a spiritual gift or answer to prayer is often accompanied by the laying on of hands.

Using a radio transmission as an analogy, if the relationship between God and us is close, then the communication lines are open and clear. If we persist in rebellion or empower the dangerous "spirit of religion," the communication eventually declines into nothing more than static. This noise is just self-made understanding. We hear only our own noisy thoughts, and in some cases become open to demonic influences. When we rebel, the signal-to-noise ratio moves from a high percentage pure signal (i.e., God's voice and promptings) to a high percentage of noise (i.e., our own thoughts). But, there is hope! If we repent, He will reestablish clear communication with us. He desires to speak clearly to us, and we just need to reorient our antennas. Repentance restores our ability to hear again. He is eager to speak. But, are we willing to listen?

God teaches us in symbolic terms to not cast our pearls before swine (see Mt. 7:6). Likewise, He doesn't cast His pearls (e.g., precious insights to His written logos Word and rhema revelation) before human "swine," who are obstinate and rebellious and not willing to obey Him. Furthermore, Jesus told His disciples to shake the dust from their sandals, if they were not welcomed by others while bringing the good news of the Gospel (see Mt. 10:14). Likewise, if we reject Him in disobedience, like the example of King Saul who lost the anointing by disobedience, why shouldn't He shake the dust from His feet metaphorically and deny us those precious life-giving insights from His written Word or direct revelation? If you want to discern His voice clearly, learn to grow in *obedience* and *prayer*.

One key to answered prayer is to know what to pray for and what not to pray for. Have we not on occasion observed people praying for things that they simply should not be requesting. Some things that people request are sins according to the Bible. Some people ask for blessings and prayer as they seek a divorce from a spouse in order to pursue a relationship with someone else whom they fancy. Yet, the written Word of God is very clear on this issue. Divorce is detestable to God. Please don't argue with what His Word says. You need not look any further for what is God's "A-plan" concerning the immovable covenant relationship of marriage between a man and woman. Some pray, "Oh God, bless my homosexual relationship." Don't be confused; homosexuality is explicitly condemned by the written Word of God (see 1 Cor. 6:9-11; Rom. 1:18-32). Have you ever heard a persistent drunk pray with words barely discernable, "Oh God, just get me out of this mess, and I'll do anything for You for the rest of my life"? It is likely that somewhere every day many are praying, "Please God, let me win the lottery." Based on His written Word, I seriously doubt that God hears many prayers like that. And still others pray that God will bless them as they pursue harmful un-biblical actions and habits, such as dishonesty, defrauding an employer, hatred, cheating on their taxes, a greedy business transaction, stealing, pornography, gossip, gluttony, abortion, fortune-telling, witchcraft, etc. Hey, there's a very long list of sins in the Bible, and we've all been guilty of more than our fair share of them.

However, we must remember that God is holy and He sees everything that we do. Fortunately, Jesus came to save *repenters* (see Lk. 13:1-5). The apostle Paul wrote to the Corinthian believers, *"And that is what some of you **were**. But you were washed, you were sanctified, you were justified in the name of the Lord Jesus Christ and by the Spirit of our God."* (1 Cor. 6:11, emphasis added). Praise Jesus that Paul referred to those believers in Corinth who formerly were involved in horrible patterns of sin as what they "were," not as what they "are." Jesus can remove the crud from our lives and set us free! We're no longer captive to what we "were." A true act of repentance results in a transformed life.

God will not work at cross purposes to His established Word and will. Too many prayers, like the examples listed above, are just plain words of selfish desires. God has already established biblical principles to help direct our lives, and we just need to be obedient to those written truths. So-called "faith" built upon selfish desires and/or presumptuous prayers is nothing more than a house of cards. It will fail. In all issues where the God-breathed Bible is explicitly clear, our personal opinions to the contrary are entirely irrelevant. Since the Bible instructs that lying, hatred, adultery, drunkenness, homosexuality, etc. are obvious sins, our opinions to the contrary do not matter before Him. We shouldn't rationalize sin. Since the Bible says that homosexuality is a sin, then it is not caused by a genetic variation. Since the Bible says that drunkenness is a sin, then it is not a disease. And, since the Bible says that lying is a sin, then it is not acceptable to lie for personal or corporate gain. Either the Bible is true, or it is not. Either it is the Word of God, or it is not. Let's be honest about these issues. Our righteous and just God will not honor prayers that run counter to His logos Word. So, we must be students of the Bible in order to grow in awareness of God's standards for acceptable behavior. We must stop praying against His revealed will in the Bible.

After we have grown in maturity and recognize obvious sins, then we have to begin to discern what to pray when we face choices within the areas of liberty and freedom (see Gal. 5). Some choices are better than others, and it takes wisdom and discernment to follow Him. We should ask for His revelation on which choices to pursue within the realm of personal liberty.

Hindrance to Effective Prayer

If you have been around the "church" for some time, you've frequently heard people ending their prayers with this tag line, "...if it be Your will, God." Almost always this is unnecessary rhetoric. This line demonstrates a lack of confidence in a prayer-answering Almighty God. Either we are praying for God's will or we are not! We shouldn't pray in doubt and then expect Him to do anything for us. The apostle James wrote about effective prayer,

If any of you lacks wisdom, he should ask God, who gives generously to all without finding fault, and it will be given to him. But when he asks, he must believe and not doubt, because he who doubts is like a wave of the sea, blown and tossed by the

wind. That man should not think he will receive anything from the Lord; he is a double-minded man, unstable in all he does (James 1:5-8).

Are we surprised that He doesn't answer prayers that end with, "...if it be Your will, God"? We haven't prayed for any specific outcome. These types of prayers are amorphous and plastic, not really asking for anything. From experience in answered prayer and observation, I honestly believe that these particular words are a hindrance to answered prayer. It is easier to steer a moving ship in a new direction that has some momentum, than it is to steer it from a dead stopped position. We just move forward to the best of our discernment and wisdom in our relationship with Him. He will nudge and prompt us when our prayers are self-serving and need to be refocused. But, in the moving forward in specific requests we will begin to receive increased revelation and clarity.

If we don't know what to pray, then either pray nothing (and I do that quite frequently), or pray asking for discernment about His will in the matter (see Jas. 1:5). Just because someone asks us to agree with her or him about a prayer request, doesn't mean that we should. We must have discernment of not only God's general will, but also His specific will and timing.

The Bible provides not only explicit commandments, but also general principles of conduct. For instance, the Book of Proverbs is filled with practical principles to help build wisdom and discernment. One of my close Christian friends is a successful businessman. He exemplifies a life of wisdom. After experiencing a painful employment problem in business early in his career, he determined that he would memorize the Book of Proverbs, which he did. That is no easy feat. Those principles, mostly from King Solomon, provide us with practical God-honoring counsel. I surely cherish my friend's wisdom, advice, and intercession. We all need close friends who are wise and knowledgeable of the Scriptures.

Wisdom and discernment become excellent tutors for our prayer lives. If we don't know what to pray, then locate a section of Scripture related to the issue at hand and then paraphrase or directly repeat Scriptures back to God. It is hard to go wrong doing that approach. God's Word is powerful, and when we are in agreement with it, then things begin to shift in the heavenly realm.

PRAYING WITH POWER

Many believers earnestly desire to have real *power* in their prayer lives. They hunger for it. They feel impotent and envious of those who seem to have it all together. They really want to see God answer them in powerful and miraculous terms. Please, listen to this advice concerning prayer and obedience. By Jesus' grace and favor, I've witnessed many answered specific prayers (and signs and miracles) in my life. According to the prophetic advice in 2000 of Mamie Jo Hunter, an elderly prophetic evangelist in Atlanta, if I neglected to keep a journal, I would forget some of these striking testimonies of answered prayers. And, if I didn't forget them perhaps some people might question their veracity. Thus, a dated journal record would exist to validate the claims and to refute any potential scoffers who lacked faith. Answered prayers and prophetic insights are very common in my life and coincidentally in the lives of many close friends around the globe. Sometimes we can exchange multiple testimonies of recent exciting events for hours.

With confidence I recommend to you that if you desire to grow in power in your prayer life, identify a prayer partner or intercessor with a "successful" pattern of answered prayer. Then, volunteer to be mentored by them. They might have the spiritual gifts of intercessor, prophetic intercessor, or miraculous works. Regardless of that individual's giftings, the caveat is this—effective prayer warriors and intercessors are extremely rare individuals in most typical Western churches!

One suggestion—you might have better odds if you can find almost any disciple from a Third World country. The odds are much greater that any such Christian foreigner already knows how to pray and live in faith. By comparison, disciples from the Third World can often put a typical Western Christian's prayers to shame. Find a devoted disciple of prayer from Nigeria, India, or China or another country and see if this is not in fact a true principle. The lack of comfort in their difficult lives draws them into a closer relationship of trust and faith in God and thus fear of the Lord. I recall listening in sheer amazement to the prayer of the young son of my friend, Pastor Oyitso Brown, the Lagos State Pastor of the Redeemed Christian Church of God in Nigeria. At the time I was preaching in Lagos, and his son was under the age of ten. That boy's confident and articulate prayer could run circles around most American Sunday school teachers in their 50's. There is no doubt that Pastor Brown and his lovely wife have instilled in their children the power of passionate prayer. I have seldom seen anything like this in the USA, with the exception of youth trained at the International House of Prayer in Kansas City, Missouri, that was founded by Mike Bickle and several prophetic colleagues. When preaching in India, it is both normal and routine to encounter passionate prayer and worship, even among the youth. Those who possess very little in life physically often have great spiritual riches and deep faith. It reminds us of the Beatitudes of Jesus in Matthew's Gospel chapter 5. So, find a disciple of Jesus from a Third World country and befriend them. You might benefit far more from them than you could possibly imagine. Just get over your possible concerns that they might want something from you, and begin to build a mutual bridge into their lives. Learn to pray as they have learned in their homelands.

It is a human tendency to think that we can bargain with God for what we desire. We are prone to "making a deal" with God in our prayers to get our will fulfilled. We think and pray, "If I do this, then He'll do that." God usually isn't a deal maker with us. He writes the rules and we must obey them. But, there are some examples in the Scriptures of His children negotiating with Him to make a deal. For instance, Abraham negotiated six times for the fate of the people of Sodom (see Gen. 18). Amos negotiated for God to relent from judgment, and He did temporarily (see Amos 7). King Hezekiah pleaded for healing and longer life, and it was granted to him (see 2 Kings 20; Is. 39). However, if you read further about what eventually happened after these prayers, you'll notice that the individuals might well have been better off to have not asked for those deviations from

God's stated original plans. The ultimate outcome of these stories seems very similar to God's stated original intentions, only delayed. These exceptions where God delivers a prophetic warning and then apparently changes His mind after people pray must be balanced by other Scriptures that say God does not change His mind. For instance, *"He who is the Glory of Israel does not lie or change His mind; for He is not a man that He should change His mind"* (1 Sam. 15:29). The take-home lesson is this—God is smarter than we are. He knows what is best, even when our prayers are well intentioned, but perhaps misled. But, He is searching for true intercessors, who will listen to Him and act on behalf of the things He is concerned about.

SUGGESTIONS FOR AN EFFECTIVE PRAYER LIFE

- Pursue fasting on occasion and with regularity. If necessary, consult a physician if you have a medical condition or any disorder or are taking medication that is likely to make it questionable to fast. The process of fasting seems difficult at first, but once you have done it a few times, you grow to appreciate the Holy Spirit power released through the process. I find that spiritual breakthroughs and revelation are more common during extended fasts. I personally prefer liquid-only, multi-day fasts, but there are many varieties of effective fasts. Replace the meal times with prayer. Let the *spirit* component within our beings grow in prominence, and may the soul and body take a "back seat" during that time.

- Recognize the authority and power of the "blood of Jesus" and speak of it. There is real power in the life-giving and redeeming blood of Jesus. This key "tip" is also very useful during spiritual warfare and/or demonic deliverance.

- As you pray, join up with others who demonstrate faith. Passionate prayer in unison with like-minded individuals is highly encouraged (see Acts 4). United prayer can result in breakthroughs in warfare and travailing prayers.

- Verbally declare your requests out loud, just as Jesus admonished, *"Have faith in God...I tell you the truth, if anyone says* to this mountain, 'Go, throw yourself into the sea,' and does not doubt in his heart but believes that what he *says* will happen, it will be done for him. Therefore I tell you, whatever you *ask* for in prayer, believe that you have received it, and it will be yours. And when you stand praying, if you hold anything against any-one, forgive him, so that your Father in heaven may forgive you your sins" (Mk. 11:22-25, emphasis added). Many of us must be retrained to declare our prayers and speak into being statements of faith. This is not only for our own benefit and maturation, but also to establish accountability and eventually a testimony before others, once the prayers have been answered. However, we must not do this in public merely in order to be noticed by others—that would just be a manifestation of pride. With that single caveat in mind, let us speak out in public prayer with boldness.

- There are various effective forms of prayer. Perhaps the least understood is "intercession," which is often referred to as "standing in the gap" between God and the issue (e.g., people, nations, events, etc.). At its core, *intercession is focused on the needs of others,* and requires a selfless attitude of service for the benefit of the purpose. It is not about "us." Intercession can also at times have the form of "warfare," where it can appear loud, passionate, and rowdy, with people laying prostrate, kneeling, standing, and pacing back and forth! The "warfare" form can be perceived with considerable uneasiness or offense by individuals lacking understanding or experience. This form is common in demonic deliverance ministry. From personal experience, I can testify that within a community of trained intercessors "mountains" can be moved! *"Where there are no oxen, the manger is empty, but from the strength of an ox comes an abundant harvest"* (Prov. 14:4). Oxen make messes. Unlike intercession, prayers can include petitions for your own needs.

- I recommend that you read books on the topics of prayer and intercession by leading authors, such as Dutch Sheets,

Jim Goll, Chuck Pierce, and the biography of Rees Howells. Learn from their vast experiences. They will provide insights to help grow this spiritual discipline.

- Model the prayers of biblical intercessors and prayer warriors, who were passionate in approaching our Father. Consider the patterns of prayers of Jesus, Daniel, Joseph, Esther, Ezra, Nehemiah, David, Paul, Moses, the woman with the hemorrhage, the blind beggar Bartimaeus, etc. Their prayers were filled with passion, faith, and courage. Many cried out (and sometimes in tears), many lay prostrate, many knelt down, many raised their hands, and many persisted until they had received the internal assurance of answered prayer. Prayers in the Bible are declared with passion and boldness. The Western Church has misled many people on what biblical passionate prayer looks and sounds like. We must move beyond the limiting concept that prayer belongs only in the box of our private "quiet times." God is stirred to action by the passionate cries of His yielded daughters and sons.

- Speak to the solution of a problem, as opposed to just restating the problem. Many church prayer groups merely list or regurgitate all of the people who have cancer, diabetes, heart problems, etc., which reinforces a negative attitude lacking hope. Where is the expectancy of God to act in response to faith? I am personally tired of viewing lengthy lists of the ill members of a church in a Sunday bulletin. Rather, speak out loud about God's revealed general or specific will in a situation via the logos Word or rhema revelation. He delights in us when we expect that He will show up at the party!

Know that Jesus and the Holy Spirit both intercede for us to the Father in Heaven. Jesus and the Holy Spirit are waging battles against satan, the accuser who stands before the Father pleading for his case against the children of God (see Rev. 12:10). Note that our holiness and righteousness directly impact the outcome of those battles. If you want your prayer life to grow and become increasingly more effective, then voluntarily remove the dirt (i.e., sin) from your life and focus on living in holiness. The dirt of your life provides satan with a legal foothold over your life, until you repent and are delivered from those patterns of sin. One of the most common examples of closely held sin is unforgiveness. This sin creates a blockage for the flow of God's grace to answer prayer.

Not all of our prayers will be Holy Spirit inspired, as there remains a measure of "us" and our personal desires left in many of our prayers. Sure, we will make mistakes, but He is more interested in our character being transformed into His likeness, than He is in whether we're always correct in our prayers. It takes practice to mature in prayer. Be willing and forgiving of yourself and others. We won't always get it right. Let's not be disillusioned when some of our prayers are not answered as we had hoped. Pastor Chris Hodges of the Church of the Highlands in Birmingham says, "Since we cannot take the credit whenever an answered prayer or miracle occurs, neither should we be embarrassed if it does not happen. Our job is just to continue to pray in faith." Chris is right on the money. Sometimes we experience answers and sometimes we don't.

I do not believe that the power to work a miracle or answer a prayer is inherent in *us*, rather it is inherent in *Him*. It depends on His willingness to act at that moment and in agreement with His Word. We do not determine when He is willing to act. For further insight on this concept please examine the gospel of John, where it frequently states that Jesus could only do that which He saw His Father doing at that time. The faith we reveal through prayer is not ours *per se*, it is *His* faith flowing through us as His conduits (see Gal. 2:20, albeit not in the NIV translation). His faith moves mountains, but our natural wimpy faith has very limited power in itself. Answered prayer is not about us, or our power, or our spiritual giftings. It is all about Him, His power, and the gifts that He has deposited within us as His servants.

Intercessors know that lesson well. Intercessors seek to dwell in the presence of God. I'm fortunate to have friends who are called and spiritually gifted as intercessors, such as Marisa Lewis, who is a gifted prophetic intercessor. She and others selflessly bring to the table during intercession an expectancy that God will in fact work on their behalf. It is exciting to pray with real intercessors.

Intercessors are seldom up front and noticed, but they are very precious in the sight of God and each of us who need their prayer support. Intercessors are like mushrooms hidden away in caves; they transform raw dirt and manure into something beautiful, delicate, and delicious! Out of the darkness they yield something useful. They are serious about what God is doing in, through, and around them. If I'm entering a spiritual warfare foxhole, I know whom I want in it with me. Send in the prophetic intercessors! They are a special gift to the Kingdom. I've grown to appreciate in the past few years that when we voluntarily enter spiritual warfare, we need them on our side. Oh God, raise up armies of prophetic intercessors in our day!

There is no room for *competition within* the Kingdom of God, as the greatest shall be the servant of the least (see Mk. 9:33-37; Mt. 18:1-5). It doesn't matter who is the conduit for His power to work in prayer or the miraculous. The point is to release God's purposes on Earth and in Heaven. Our prayers mobilize angels under His command to cause things to happen, and it doesn't matter who gets the credit. We competitive Westerners seldom understand this concept. We want all the affirmation and accolades that we can muster from others, as if by our own power the prayers are answered...that is foolish. There is no room for competition within the Kingdom, because we should all be on the same team.

Prayers are answered by His power, and we're just the conduits making the requests. He gets the credit. Who cares through whom our Holy Spirit's power flows? It isn't about us; it's about Him. If we get upset that God's power is flowing through someone else instead of through us, then we have a problem with pride and/or envy. The objective in prayer is for His will to be established (e.g., that the captives be set free). It isn't for us to merely feel good about ourselves vis-à-vis other believers. Remember, our righteous judgment by the living God will be based upon our love and obedience to use the talents and gifts granted to us for His plans. It will have very little to do with the plans God had for other individuals. We should stop comparing ourselves to others in a competitive mode, and just become the salt and light that He has called us as individuals to fulfill. Let all that we do and say be according to *His* will, not our will. Jesus instructed us to do that in the model prayer He offered, "...*Your kingdom come, Your will be done on earth as it is in heaven*" (Mt. 6:10. emphasis added). It is not about you, or me, or us collectively in a local church. It is about Him. It isn't about our desires. It is about His sovereign will, plans, strategies, and timing. The essence of answered prayer is to know what and when to pray, as revealed to us by the Holy Spirit through the logos Word and rhema revelation. It is really that simple! Jesus said, "*If you remain in Me and My words remain in you, ask whatever you wish, and it will be given you. This is to My Father's glory, that you bear much fruit, showing yourselves to be My disciples...Then the Father will give you whatever you ask in My name*" (Jn. 15:7-8,16).

How do we pray when there appear to be opposing sides to an issue or multiple possibilities, including when different Christians pray for opposing outcomes? People ask us to agree in prayer for all sorts of things. Some requests we can agree with, such as those in agreement with the general or specific will of God. Some requests we must not agree with (i.e., if we know God's will is not in agreement with the request). Do not permit people to manipulate you into praying against God's will, lest you join into their folly.

We must learn to know what to pray for, what to not pray for (i.e., abstain), and what to pray against! That's where both the logos Word and rhema revelation intersect in the picture. By default, there is no harm in praying that His will and His "A-plan" be established. Beyond that, does the particular individual who is praying have a solid and highly reliable track record of clearly discerning the revelation of God and the will of God?

PERSONAL BIASES INFLUENCE OUR OBJECTIVITY

A large number of Caucasian believers in the USA consider themselves politically as Republicans, because they perceive this political party as "closely" aligned to the Bible. At times, some of them voice Republican political ideologies as if those positions are synonymous with God's will in a specific situation. Some Republican ideals and agendas are God-honoring, but some are not. It might shock some people to know that God is not a Republican. Neither is He a "Big D" Democrat, which some African-Americans tend to believe. Some Democratic issues are God-honoring, but not all. As a matter of fact, some Democrats have agendas that are appalling biblically, such as advocating for so-called "free choice," an intentionally deceptive term that includes abortion on demand, and pro-homosexual rights. Some Republican issues appear to lack understanding of the heart of the Father for the widow, fatherless, alien, orphan, poor, homeless, and the oppressed, as exemplified in Isaiah 58 and Matthew 25. Neither is God a communist, nor a socialist for that matter. Let the entire teachings of the Bible be supreme over individual political preferences and opinions. We are first of all called as believers in the King of kings, and are therefore primarily citizens of His Kingdom. Therefore, political affiliations and beliefs should be subordinate to the whole counsel of Scripture. Oh, how God desires that Christians and Jews today would understand this critical distinction.

People tend to package God into a box of their own limited understanding and cultural preferences, including political ideologies and systematic theologies. That is wrong, or at least very limiting. It is quite helpful to have traveled extensively around the globe. In so doing, we develop a heightened awareness of our limited insights and cultural blinders. We begin to see our variety of Judeo-Christian beliefs and preferences in a broader light. If you live isolated in only one community all your life, your perspective on who God is and what He does is very limited, and thus will be further from the truth.

For instance, in the freedom-conscious USA, there is an inherent mental filter of independent thinking (e.g., individuality, personal rights, independence from parental authority) that affects most people. However, in many parts of Asia, the plurality and communal goodwill is held in high esteem. Over there, one would seldom dare challenge the authority of parents and local "elders." These two "opposing" cultural norms contain certain elements of biblical truth. But, both are prone to error if too highly elevated or imbalanced relative to other biblical truths. Thus, in the USA, love of freedom in the extreme can lead to rebellion against God-established authorities, and in Asia the respect for parents in the extreme can lead to idolatry, in which ancestors are worshiped.

We are routinely blinded to our own biases, and it sometimes takes an outside perspective of comparison to illuminate our limited understanding. Biblical truth can withstand cultural distinctions and diversity without fear. Hallelujah! The genuine expressions of Judeo-Christian truths are very diverse in different communities and races around the globe. For instance, I have a friend, Randy Woodley, who is a Native American and author of *Living in Color*. He appreciates diverse expressions of biblical truths, yet within the context of American Indian cultural ceremonies and traditions. So long as the truths of the Bible remain intact and do not encroach upon syncretism (i.e., compromising biblical truth for the sake of cultural practices), then let us show liberty and embrace various forms of expression of these truths. I am grateful for the courage of men and women, such as Randy and Edith Woodley, who desire to demonstrate Judeo-Christian beliefs using culturally relevant examples, so as to reach peoples who would otherwise consider Judeo-Christianity offensive or irrelevant. As another example Hudson Taylor did "similar" things to reach the peoples of China with the gospel.

Western "Christians" have so limited the permutations and possibilities of what is "acceptable" to God. But, He is not at all limited by our self-imposed limitations of expression of genuine worship (see Gal. 5). One can prepare a huge list of Western concepts that have defined for Christianity what is "appropriate" contextually. Yet, none of these things are truly and exclusively biblical concepts, and some are contrary to the Scriptures either explicitly or implicitly. Just for your personal enlightenment, consider whether the following items that are commonplace examples in Western churches are biblical or not:

• Services are held in a square or rectangular building.

- The building is called a "church" and the people are called "members."

- An individual pastor is *the* leader of a local church.

- A minister standing up on a stage in front of the "laymen."

- "Worship" means to sing songs, and frequently aided by organ music.

- Choirs with individuals wearing special robes.

- Stained-glass windows and steeples as features of the building.

- Celebration of Christmas and national patriotic holidays.

- "Acceptable" dress codes.

- Services that are run according to a clock, for instance lasting only one hour.

- Democratic-style voting by "members."

- "Hiring" a pastor, and especially from outside of the congregation.

- Services held on Sunday morning (vs. the Friday evening of the Jewish Shabbat).

- The frequency and conduct of "communion" services.

- Services that are programmed based on a written "liturgy" or schedule.

- Replacement of all "Jewish" holidays from the calendar.

- Being quiet equates with being reverent to God.

- Demonstrating passionate expressions "in church" is discouraged as emotionalism.

- The order of services such as "stand up, sing a hymn, sit down, read, and kneel."

Just for the thrill of the experience, may I suggest that you take out your Bible and attempt to carefully defend any of these common practices of many churches.

PROPHETIC VOICES HELP US HEAR FROM GOD

We need to know who are the reliable prophetic and discerning voices within the Church. The Hebrew prophet Amos instructs us that, *"Surely the Sovereign Lord does **nothing** without revealing His plan to His servants the prophets"* (Amos 3:7, emphasis added). And, the Lord said, *"Shall I hide from Abraham what I am about to do?"* (Gen. 18:17). Even when God is about to do something "new," there are some reliable apostolic and/or prophetic individuals who can discern what is about to happen in advance, as God reveals it to those He has chosen. God engages His prophets as part of His "advance team" in the process of releasing revelations and new movements.

Personal preferences, desires, and agendas taint our ability to hear clearly the rhema revelation of God. So, I would rather trust one highly reliable prophet (or prophetic-discerning disciple) than a thousand "believers" with good intentions and more limited prophetic awareness. The prophet's role is to speak the heart of the Holy Spirit's intentions like a watchman on a tower looking out for warning signs (see Ezek. Chapters 3, 33). It is not the prophet's responsibility whether individuals respond in one way or the other. The prophet must simply declare and warn if necessary of what he or she knows or has discerned is true based on the rhema revelation that is consistent with the logos Word.

Many individuals have not learned how to discern the rhema revelation of God for today's issues. Many people have been misled by the "spirit of religion" and/or are operating from a position of presumption in their own understanding. It doesn't matter one ounce what anyone of us thinks. Our opinions don't matter! God's revelation is what is entirely important. Some individuals within the Church think that they hear from God, but they are self-deceived. They usually have telltale flaws in their character. I've encountered it at various times. It has been uncomfortable to have to point out to them the truth revealed by the Holy Spirit, whether they like it or not. Reliable prophets are given to the Church to help guide the plurality of believers in the Body into wisdom and discernment. Prayer that is answered isn't about a "popularity vote." It doesn't matter what a majority of Christians think or the majority of ministers think. Some individuals in the Church are not clearly hearing from God. Some of them are quite vocal with opinions contrary to the will of God. What the Church needs is clear prophetic revelation to lead decisions and prayer.

I have enjoyed the privilege of becoming a friend to a large number of God-honoring and reliable prophetic individuals. These men and women have received spiritual giftings and callings for the building up of the Body of Christ (see Eph. 4:11-13). These prophetic voices can help provide guidance to others. For instance, consider two examples—Mamie Jo Hunter and Dennis Arnold. I have benefited from knowing Mrs. Hunter, a lovely elderly Christian woman in Atlanta, Georgia. She has had a lifetime prophetic and evangelistic ministry of impact, under the banner of "The Gospel Carrier" ministry. She has been highly precise and accurate with regard to the revelations of the Holy Spirit since she was a teenage girl. I have heard many of her testimonies of prophecies and faith, which were confirmed by a witness to the events.

She has spoken prophecies to me about my future and God's plans for me to impact the world. For instance, one time I phoned Mamie Jo to inform her about an exciting encounter I had the prior day with another prophetic woman, whom I had just met. That woman had declared a specific Bible passage that applied to my calling. However, before I could complete my remarks and state the precise Bible passage (i.e., Rev. 3:7-13), Mamie Jo politely interrupted to mention that she had shared the exact same Scripture to someone else the prior day, too. She "knew" in her spirit what I was about to say, even before the words left my mouth.

Mamie Jo mentored a dear friend of mine, Dennis Arnold, a prophetic Gospel singer-songwriter from Alabama. As a small boy, Dennis had one of the most remarkable and miraculous testimonies of salvation and healing from paralyzing polio, bar none. In January

2000, I met Dennis through a miraculous encounter with his son, Jeremy, who was a stranger to me at the time. God instructed me to go to the bank on a Saturday morning, and to give away some money that morning to "poor strangers." So, I went to the bank's ATM to withdraw some cash, accompanied by my three youngest children. On the ride to the bank I remarked to my daughter, Catherine, that I believed that God wanted our family to help struggling Christian musicians and artists, including financially. Jeremy arrived at the bank at precisely the same time, but he didn't appear to my eyes of sight to be poor. He was a handsome, well-dressed, suburban young man, and not at all what I had envisioned. I was looking for an unkempt homeless man or woman with tattered clothing. However, I was prompted by the Holy Spirit to give this "poor stranger" some cash, even though I had to believe that he was poor by the eyes of faith. After doing so, in response he gave me a CD recording of his father's songs without explanation.

I learned the following day that Jeremy had no money because he was assisting with his father's music ministry. Dennis had told Jeremy that God would provide for his needs, and to go to the bank just to see if God wouldn't act on his behalf. Jeremy was shocked at what I did at the prompting of the Holy Spirit. All he did was show up at the bank, and my family handed him the money for his immediate need from our bank account. It was a delight to subsequently meet Dennis Arnold, a man of great faith, who has endured many years of great difficulties and disappointments since childhood. But, Dennis is still holding onto his faith in Jesus. He is a victorious overcomer with an anointing of abundant love for healing body and soul. Spending time with Dennis is like hanging out with Jesus. Oh God, may you bless Dennis abundantly in this life and in the eternity to come! God, use examples such as Mamie Jo Hunter and Dennis Arnold to demonstrate that Jesus is alive and well and that the Holy Spirit is still speaking to those who have ears to hear!

Prior to prayer we should first discern what God's will is, and not pray about things that are not His will. If the issue is confusing or conflicted and requires prophetic revelation or insight, then surround yourself by at least one experienced and precise prophetic individual. Precision is hitting the mark exactly, whereas accuracy is related to how consistent you are over time. One can be highly precise on occasion but not accurate, and you can also be accurate without high precision. We should seek out prophetic individuals that are both precise and accurate, and pray for God's protection and continued revelation in and through their lives.

One piece of valuable advice—don't hastily speak against the words of a God-honoring prophet, unless there is solid reason to doubt the reliability of that particular individual. I wouldn't want to bet very often against a precise and accurate prophet. We should grant a prophet the benefit of the doubt and not mock God's anointed, which is a dangerous thing.

When asked to pray, follow the Spirit's promptings in obedience, regardless of what someone asks you to do in prayer. If possible, check to see if it resonates with the prophetic revelation of a reliable prophet's words. A reliable prophet's revelation should always be considered with the highest regard, especially vis-à-vis someone else's "non-prophetic" opinion. A true prophet's revelations cannot be negated by anyone with a contrary opinion. It doesn't matter what others think. A genuine prophet is entrusted with valuable information that most believers don't possess. Frankly most believers can't comprehend it, because they haven't walked in the prophet's anointing and gifting. Thus, it is good to know who the reliable prophets and apostles are within the Body of Christ, and who the counterfeit "posers and pretenders" are that should be disregarded and rejected. It takes spiritual discernment and training to do this well. (For more on prophets and apostles, see Chapter 10.)

Some of us don't need to spend so much time praying until we're blue in the face, because, "*...your Father knows what you need before you ask Him*" (Mt. 6:8). Some approach God as if He is a magician, a genie in a bottle, or a Santa Claus, who is there just to grant their selfish requests and long lists. Our natural hearts are filled with corrupt and selfish thoughts and desires. We need balance in our approaches to prayer. Please spend more time in singing praises to Jesus and adoring Him. He wants us to enjoy being in relationship. He'll take care of our needs.

As we begin to pray, it is good to enter His courts with praise and thanksgiving (see Phil. 4:6). For instance, in Second Chronicles 20, worship in song preceded a great battle victory. King David recorded for our benefit many Psalms of praise that can be used during prayer. God is earnestly seeking those who will worship Him in *Spirit* and in *truth*. He desires to answer their prayers.

Reinhard Bonnke wrote in *Faith: The Link with God's Power,* "Faith without prayer is possible, but prayer without faith is useless. Jesus said, '*When you pray, believe*' (Mark 11:24). It is the prayer of faith that is effective." Many and perhaps most believers when asked would likely reply that their prayers often seem ineffective and largely useless. Perhaps they haven't captured the essential truths of what real faith-led prayer is about. God's power to work in our seemingly impossible situations is released by our prayers of faith in passion. We must believe for Him to do it on our behalf in accordance with His Word, and then we must be prepared to take additional steps of action in faith as prompted by the Holy Spirit.

Chapter Six

QUESTIONS

1. What level of "success" would you rate your prayer life (from a minimum of 1 to a maximum of 10)?

2. List the most amazing testimonies of answered prayer in your life.

3. Can you define any differences between intercession, prophetic intercession, and other forms of prayer?

4. Patterns of sin quench the Holy Spirit's willingness to work through us. Do you ever sense that God is judging you for past failures and sins, or that He is displeased with you? Do you believe that you are unworthy and guilty about sin patterns in your life?

5. Which one of the principles of prayer listed in this chapter do you intend to implement to improve your personal prayer life?

6. To better understand God and pray more effectively, consider using His distinct biblical names, for instance: *El Shaddai,* the all-sufficient nourishing God; *El Elyon,* the most high God; *Adonai,* the Lord; The God of Abraham, Isaac, and Jacob. Unfortunately, our translations of the Bible typically reduce the richness of the multiple names of God as either the generic "Lord" or "God." Research the names of God in the Bible and ponder how each can be effectively used as a tool in prayer.

Chapter Seven

PERSONAL TESTIMONIES
OF PRAYING FAITH

*They overcame him [satan] by the blood of the Lamb [Jesus]
and by the word of their* **testimony**; *they did not love their
lives so much as to shrink from death* (Revelation 12:11,
emphasis added).

*Therefore I glory in Christ Jesus in my service to God. I will not
venture to speak of anything except what Christ has accomplished through me in leading the Gentiles to obey God by what
I have said and done—by the power of signs and miracles,
through the power of the Spirit...* (Romans 15:17-19).

This Scripture provides us with one of the greatest tools for spiritual warfare—testimonies of what God has done supernatu-
rally for you and through you. Throughout the Bible, God tells His
followers to build altars of remembrance to the great and mighty
acts that He performed for them. We likewise should build figurative "altars of remembrance" with our oral or written testimonies.

For several decades and especially since 1997 God has moved
powerfully in my life on a consistent basis providing me with
many examples of testimonies of answered prayer and miracles as
a result of a life surrendered in faith. I share the following selected
examples for your encouragement and to stimulate you on to further maturity in the Lord. I am nothing. But, by the grace of God
I have been engrafted into the faith lineage of Abraham. These

115

testimonies are the result of a life progressively surrendered and yielded to His will, and are not a reflection of my personal will, which is inherently corrupt.

I do not share the following examples to boast about personal accomplishments or to draw attention to "self." On the contrary, we must follow the biblical mandate to all believers to be humble, yet *boast* in knowing Him (see Jer. 9:23-24; 2 Cor. 10,11) and in the cross of Jesus Christ through which we are saved (see Gal. 6:14). In some examples, the faith of other individuals who have positively impacted my life are noted. Testimonies of a transformed life in Jesus are powerful weapons that we should use as a skilled warrior for the King of kings. When we give testimonies of God's prior work and miracles (see Ps. 77:11-15; 145:4-6; Acts 14:27; 21:17-20), we also remind our adversary that all authority in Heaven and on Earth rests in Jesus, through whom the act was accomplished. He gets the glory, not us. Testimonies are very powerful weapons!

ENGLAND

There are a few individuals who stand out from all the rest as having substantially impacted my life. In 1986-1988, John and Marie Manwell attended a small group Bible study in our mid-terraced row home at 66 Walpole Road, South Woodford in London, England. John is a proverbial sold-out-for-Jesus type of disciple. He is a 100 percent committed man of God with tangible evidence of genuine faith in action.

Although he is tenderhearted and encouraging, he is also bold, intense, provocative, and willing to take a stand for what he believes, even in the face of opposition. John fears God Almighty more than man. During our Monday night meetings of seven young married couples, John challenged my faith and evangelical doctrine, and helped introduce to me the filling power of the Holy Spirit. He is an unusual man. Once he even shaved his head and shocked everyone at church. Maybe John wondered what it was like to be bald just like Elisha (see 2 Kings 2:23), or maybe he had taken some vow before God. I don't know why he did it. John certainly takes the path less traveled as a disciple of Jesus.

In 1987, John brought an audiocassette tape to our Monday meeting by the German evangelist, Reinhard Bonnke, of whom I hadn't heard of previously. The tape had a simple message in which Reinhard asked, "Do *you* believe in miracles today?" Prior to that moment, I had been a serious student of the Bible for the past decade and had reasonable knowledge of the logos written Word of God. But, prior to that time I hadn't really given much thought to the power of the Holy Spirit to work in signs, wonders, and miracles—the supernatural evidences of the Holy Spirit at work through the lives of Christians. Well, that night in my spirit I replied, "Yes, I do believe in miracles today!" Then, I witnessed a small faith miracle that evening concerning a neighbor, who phoned during our meeting.

It is an understatement that John Manwell and Reinhard Bonnke have impacted my life. Reinhard is one of the most powerful evangelists and miracle workers in the world today. He routinely preaches to audiences in Africa approaching or exceeding one million at one place. True to his faith and direct style, John paid out of his pocket to rent a bus (or "hire a coach" as they say in the UK) to take his friends and family from London to hear Reinhard speak in Birmingham, England. I was privileged to ride up to Birmingham and hear Reinhard speak live for the first time. What developed within my spirit was a graphical image or goal that I, too, would some day have an anointing in global ministry with some similarities to Mr. Bonnke's. I would stand on stages before large audiences (and especially of dark-skinned individuals) to share the Word of God in evangelism and exhortation. I am beginning to see that those days of prophetic fulfillment are happening in the current season and the days ahead. I expect this to happen by faith, even though I am a scientist-entrepreneur by profession. I have a passion for prophetic preaching and leadership training, but I currently earn my living by other "secular" means.

John Manwell and his wife, Marie, and I have a special spiritual revelation connection. Through the work of the Holy Spirit, we often will sense things in our spirits at the same time, though we're separated by 4,000 miles and an ocean. For instance, several years ago I woke up in the middle of the night in Alabama to phone them to say, "I believe that God wants you to read Joshua 5 now. You're about to enter a *verdant* land." John was surprised to hear me say the term "verdant," as he had just looked it up in the dictionary that morning in the UK prior to my call. I was surprised because the term is not commonplace in my vocabulary, although I know the term's meaning of lush and green.

In the Spring of 2002, Marie was watching President George W. Bush on the television in their home and center of their ministry, termed "The Well." She knew of our collective prayers that I would appear before the president. So, she went up to the TV and touched it saying, "God, please send Tom to meet with President Bush soon." Within a few days I had sent a joyous e-mail report to them indicating that I had been invited to meet the President the following Wednesday in the White House.

In 2003 John took a decorative prophetic prayer rod/staff (created in Birmingham, Alabama) with him as he traveled to London to make prophetic declarations. He gave me advanced notice by e-mail to keep a careful watch on the news out of London that week. Within a couple days of prophetically striking the ground with that rod in Parliament, there was a "surprising" power outage in much of London. Ironically that very morning I had sent him an e-mail message with a satellite photograph of the effects of a major power outage in Northeastern USA shortly before this incident. I had simply asked in the e-mail message, "Is this a sign of more to follow?" Within hours of my message being sent, there was a major blackout in London and within a couple months another "surprising" major power blackout in Italy. God has been warning John for more than a decade that He is about to shake the nations of the Earth (see Hag. 2:21-22; Heb. 12:25-29; Hab. 1:5-11). We need to heed this warning. Everything that can be shaken, will be shaken! And, the Church will be shaken, first. If you have not responded obediently and have not been refined by this current season of shaking, then you likely won't be ready when the really hard times hit in the days ahead!

These exchanges of prophetic words and occurrences are commonplace in our trans-Atlantic prophetic relationship. When

I first returned to the USA after leaving England in 1988, John sent to me a subscription of *Prophecy Today*, a UK-based magazine, to encourage me. I believe he did this as a declaration by faith that God had a special prophetic ministry for me in the days ahead. Then in 1999, John encouraged me to listen to the tape ministry of Dr. Howard Morgan, a Jewish believer in Jesus as the Jewish Messiah. Howard is an apostolic-prophetic leader from Atlanta, Georgia. He has since made a number of contributions to my understanding concerning Jewish roots, the Kingdom of God, and prophetic-apostolic leadership. Howard has become a friend and co-laborer. I recommend Howard Morgan's ministry and teaching tapes.

For your information, of the seven couples in that small group in London in the late 80's, most have ministries at present. John and Marie Manwell minister in Liverpool and occasionally in Africa. My other close friend, Paul Griffiths, and his wife, Diane, minister in Ormskirk near Liverpool and occasionally in Bangladesh. Rob and Sandra Hooks minister through London City Missions. Ray and Sally King minister to youth in Bournemouth and occasionally in Korea. And, the other two couples remain active in our former evangelical church in South Woodford. Many of these friends have visited and ministered with us in the USA on occasion. It is now evident that God had begun to weave a fabric of global impact and destiny into the hearts of the young couples attending a small home group in London in the late 1980's. Let us not despise the days of small beginnings (see Zech. 4:10), for with diligence in due season the fruit will be revealed.

STOPPING A TORNADO

In 2000, I was on the phone at work late in the evening, speaking with Mamie Jo Hunter. As a result, I was late arriving at a theatre performance at Vestavia Hills High School. The auditorium was filled with perhaps 600+ people. As I arrived, I parked on the hill overlooking the school as it rained. I was then led by the Holy Spirit to remain in my car and not enter the high school, even though my oldest daughter, Catherine, had a role in the play. Rather, I raised my hands in prayer, similar to Moses when he prayed as Joshua fought against the Amalekites (see Ex. 17:8-16). That evening I prayed repeatedly a very simple and specific prayer, "God, do not let a tornado strike this building tonight!" Yet, no warning siren had sounded, the rain was not particularly concerning, nor had any mention of a tornado been on the radio as I drove the short distance to the school from my office. I used my mobile phone to call my wife, Laura, to tell her that I sensed something and was remaining in my car to pray. (This served as an independent advance confirmation.) Well, I continued to repeatedly pray that one-liner, "God, do not let a tornado strike this building tonight!" Note that I'm quite familiar with tornadic activity having lived in Kansas, Texas, and Alabama the majority of my life. I have personally seen many of them from a safe distance, and even had my first home hit by a tornado in June 1981, only a few weeks after Laura and I were married.

Amazingly, approximately 20 minutes later I witnessed a remarkable sight even though it was dark and raining. A fierce, horizontal, pounding wind and torrential rain suddenly hit the back of my car and shook it. The wind was driving forward toward the high school in the direction I was looking from my driver's seat. Intense flashes of light emanated momentarily from immediately behind the school. There were power lines and transformers emitting purple-blue sparks resembling welding arcs. Then, the electricity to the entire region failed, and I stopped praying. I knew I had completed my task. Shortly thereafter emergency sirens sounded and a local fire truck was mobilized. I then took my flashlight and headed into the darkened high school.

I later learned that the Buckhead subdivision of homes immediately behind the high school had been hit by a tornado at that precise time. The cyclone had stopped literally within hundreds of yards of the school. I was an eyewitness to some of its effects. One lesson learned—I had a choice to enter the school upon arrival to watch my daughter's play, but I yielded to the promptings of the Holy Spirit and was used as a conduit of prophetic prayer in advance of an incident that God Almighty knew was about to occur. Had I not prayed, the consequences could perhaps have been quite serious for the large crowd assembled in the auditorium, including my precious oldest daughter. The Kingdom of God uses prophetic intercessors, who serve as "watchmen" for the benefit of others (see Ezek. 3 and 33).

One additional note: It is remarkable that I have had numerous dreams throughout my life since early childhood in which a tornado strikes a community. In each of the different scenarios, I am always there helping prevent casualties while the tornado is destroying the area. So, in a practical sense, I have seen that type of dream literally fulfilled before my eyes. One postscript worth noting, whirlwinds (i.e., tornados or cyclones) are mentioned in the Bible as instruments of the Sovereign Lord used in the lives of Job (see Job 1:18-22) and Elijah (see 2 Kings 2).

IN THE WHITE HOUSE

In December 2000 to early January 2001, I became aware within my spirit that I would be invited to the White House to meet with President George W. Bush. However, I didn't know anyone working in the White House or his cabinet, which would be established following the inauguration. As has been my custom for the past several years, I had recorded in my journals that I believed that I would have some part in influencing President Bush in the White House, although I was not yet sure why or how it would come to pass. In faith, I just believed it and started declaring it to many people.

Then in March 2001 I had a remarkable conversation with a woman seated next to me on a plane leaving Birmingham. As Janice Henry prepared to sit down, she placed her Bible on her seat. I looked at her and said, "We'll have plenty to discuss on this flight," to which she replied, "Are you the reason I missed my flight today?" I sensed that I might have some spiritual role to play in her situation, as I often pray that God will give me encounters with strangers on plane rides.

Parenthetically, it is amusing that I once had a German woman, sitting next to me on a flight returning from Europe, reach over and literally pinch me asking, "Are you real or are you an angel?" What I had been sharing with her she perceived was like "reading her mail" from her perspective. It was stirring up in her some serious questions about her presumptions about her relationship with God, or rather the lack of a real relationship. She asked me many questions about the Bible, and amazingly I had just completed preaching from each of the key Scriptures that addressed her needs. At the end of the flight she thanked me and said, "Before meeting you I thought I knew what it meant to be a Christian, but now you've made me aware that it is something entirely different than I had presumed." May we always be used to reach people we encounter every day.

Now, returning to the discussion with Janice. After a few minutes of conversation, she looked at me and asked, "What are you praying for? I want to record it in my prayer list for you, and be in agreement with you." I replied that I believed that God would arrange for me to be invited to meet President Bush in the White House soon, although I didn't know any of the details. President Bush is reported to be a genuine Bible-reading believer. I know that God has given me an anointing to influence governmental and business leaders around the globe for the sake of the Kingdom of God in prayer, in person, and in declared words. Surprisingly, she replied, "Oh, that's easy. Perhaps I can arrange that." In surprise I asked, "Why do you say that?" She followed, "I'm from his hometown of Midland, Texas. My husband is an acquaintance of the Bush family and a friend to a member of the President's Cabinet." This flight was also noteworthy because of extreme turbulence, and Janice and I prayed together for safety while traveling on that jet.

I doubt that Janice actually opened the door for me to the White House. But, she did specifically confirm to me that I was believing the truth about my destiny. I knew I was going to somehow impact President G.W. Bush, even though I knew no one in the White House. You just can't arrange to get yourself invited to meet with the world's most powerful man! That is, unless you are willing to donate a truckload of money for a political campaign—that might open the "back door." After Janice's "confirmation" I continued to pray and write in my journal that God would open the door for me at the White House.

Then on Palm Sunday in March 2002, as I preached in three large churches in Kerala, India, I declared to several thousand people, "Any day now the White House is going to call, and I'll be invited to meet with President Bush." One of the host pastors that morning, who had never met me until after I finished preaching at "his" local church (note that churches do not belong to a pastor), is a man of substantial influence in India and around the globe. KC John is a leader of thousands of churches in India. As I preached, he said that the Holy Spirit spoke audibly to him, "Tom is a spiritual statesman [to the nations]" which he reported to me during lunch later that day (see Jere. 1:5). He then said (in paraphrase), "When you mentioned the invitation to the White House by faith, it is a done deal!"

I returned to the US and within less than two weeks I e-mailed KC John to inform him that I had just received a phone call from the White House saying, "Dr. Dooley, this is the White House Office of the Public Liaison. President Bush has kindly requested that you come to the White House next Wednesday for a meeting." Hallelujah! The following Wednesday I not only visited the White House, but I also gave a presentation at a U.S. Senate briefing in support of a bioethics bill sponsored by Senator Sam Brownback to ban all forms of human cloning. God, continue to bless and elevate Sam Brownback of Kansas for his obedience to your Word and for defending the lives of the unborn and the nation of Israel.

After leaving the Senate briefing, I arrived inside the White House and was escorted into the Blue Room for a private meeting with the President along with perhaps nine other "invited" guests, including some key Judeo-Christian ministry leaders (e.g., Joni Eareckson Tada) and TV personalities (e.g., Patricia Heaton, the co-star of *Everybody Loves Raymond*). I spoke to President Bush face-to-face briefly and indicated my appreciation for his "new" position in opposition to human cloning, and his support for the nation of Israel, and mentioned that I pray for him often. It was an honor to dialog with him, albeit briefly. Note that the two issues I mentioned to him were revealed to my spirit 15 months earlier as critical for the Bush legacy. These two things would define his presidency (i.e., the definition of the start of human life, and his wholehearted support for Israel and the Jewish people). It was remarkable to stand there in front of the most powerful man on Earth in terms of political, military, and economic strengths, as a direct answer to a faith declaration

15 months earlier. After the Blue Room meeting, I was escorted by a military guard into a packed East Room press conference where I was taken to my seat on the front row—a chair that even had my name on it, as a guest of honor. While in the White House, I was fortunate to meet with some well-known Judeo-Christian leaders and authors, such as Chuck Colson.

There is another curious incident that happened on that day. While in the East Room, I declared a specific blessing over Senator Bill Frist of Tennessee. I had heard him speak in the US Capitol during one of my prior trips to DC, during which I had previously prayed within the Capitol building. While standing with the senator I declared a simple prayer resembling these words, "May God bless you and *elevate you* at this time." Earlier in the Spring of 2002, Senator Frist had been considered by most political observers as just one of many junior-ranking senators of limited influence, of which there are a total of 100 members of the Senate. Well, within the next year he surprisingly leapfrogged other higher-ranking senators and took over as the top-ranking leader of the majority (Republican) party of the US Senate. He has ascended to a very influential leadership position as the leader of the majority party of the Senate, considered by some political observers to be the second or third most powerful position in Washington behind the President (and the Secretary of State during most administrations). I continue to pray that Senator Frist will be obedient to God's logos and rhema revelation, and not be merely another politician pursuing power on Capitol Hill.

I know that God opened the door to the White House and US Senate briefing as a result of a faith declaration. By the way, while President G.W. Bush was still active as Governor of Texas and before he announced that he was running in the primaries to become the Republican nominee for President, I sensed that he was destined to become President. I just knew it in my spirit, and I had told people about that impression years before he became President.

May God Almighty continue to bless President Bush as he seeks to restore respect, authority, and Judeo-Christian truth to the USA. May God's will prevail in the two issues of critical importance for his presidency, and thus receive the intended blessings. May

President Bush discern who is providing him with God-honoring advice and may he flee from error. May those numerous advisors around the President providing un-biblical advice be removed. May President Bush remain a humble servant to God Almighty and thus further the Kingdom of God on Earth. May God Almighty transform the lives of his two daughters, who I suspect weigh heavily on his heart, and establish God's purposes for their destinies.

I also pray that President G.W. Bush abstain from declaring blessing over the religion of Islam. President Bush, likely under the influence of his advisors and speechwriters, has erred by declaring repeatedly that, "Islam is a religion of peace." Many objective observers of history do not agree with this assertion. Islam operates through the power of the *spirit of religion*. Islam desires to lead its observers into submission of burdensome religious traditions, and these activities do not lead toward peace or freedom. Many signs indicate that many Islamists seek to dominate the world by oppressive force. The true *Prince of Peace* is found only in Jesus. The spiritual freedom of the true gospel of Jesus Christ (see Gal. 5) is not part of Islam. Jesus came to set us free, not to enslave us to *any* religion. May Jesus set free all those who are bound by the spirit of religion, whether it be Islam, Judaism, Hinduism, or so-called "Christianity."

Our words have meanings, and we are accountable for them. The President of the United States and the leaders of all nations need to declare blessings over the *God of Abraham, Isaac, and Jacob* (Israel), if they desire for God's favor to follow them. The words of leaders of nations have both earthly and heavenly implications. God, lead our nations' leaders.

NATIONAL GOVERNMENTS AND POLITICIANS

By God's grace He has anointed me with a measure of revelation and insight regarding some governmental officials, regions, and issues around the globe (see Jere. 1:5). I know that the Holy Spirit has led me in prayer and declarations pertaining to the prophetic destinies of the state of Alabama, the United States, and several other foreign countries.

But, before sharing some examples (besides the meetings with President Bush and Senator Frist), it is worth noting that it can be quite frustrating dealing with politicians and lobbyists. I've been intimately involved in several non-profit organizations and advocacy of policies at the community, state, or federal levels. It often takes a "spine" to stand up. For every God-honoring insight that you firmly hold, there will be opposition from someone. When stirred by the Holy Spirit to take action, we must make the commitment to pursue the *truth in love,* and to pursue *good* in the particular issue.

I continue to learn "up close" that politics is about *power* at its core, and to a lesser extent the subordinate issues of *votes, money,* and *influence.* There are few genuinely altruistic individuals of integrity deeply involved in politics. Most political people have strong egos and agendas, and those agendas usually involve achieving, maintaining, and growing power. Yet, as a disciple of Jesus, I know that the Scriptures admonish us, "...*not by* [our] *might, nor by* [our] *power, but by My Spirit says the Lord Almighty*" (Zech. 4:6b). That is where we are to gather our strength. It is not from political victories. Whether we win or lose a policy battle is not the issue; we are to do what is truthful and righteous before our Creator.

Some Christians believe that they are to have nothing to do with the government, advocacy, or voting. I believe that we should disagree with this position based on biblical precedence and patterns (e.g., Rom. 13); and to the contrary we should be active in prayer, voting, and advocacy. Was not God intimately involved in sending his prophets to speak into the lives of numerous kings and rulers of Israel, Judah, and surrounding lands? Consider Jonah sent to speak to the rulers over Nineveh in hostile Assyria. Consider Joseph, Moses, and Aaron sent to speak to the pharaohs in Egypt. Consider the profound impact of Esther, Deborah, Daniel, Joshua, Elijah, Ezra, and Nehemiah in both foreign and domestic governments. Was not the sovereign God intimately involved in anointing Saul and David as kings at the hands of one of His prophets, Samuel? Was not God intimately involved in placing Jesus and Paul before the governing Roman rulers and courts? There are numerous cases in our Scriptures. In view of the pattern of this overwhelming evidence, it is difficult to envision a solid biblical argument to the contrary. (However, this is not to suggest that Jesus came to earth to be a politician.)

Nowhere in Scripture are we called to monastic separation! We are to be in the world, but not of it. We should resemble resident "aliens." Too many of us Christians want to get off the planet too quickly, ironically while Jesus wants to go in the opposite direction. He desires to live out His will for the Kingdom through us while we're still resident on this planet. If we are silent or withdrawn, what will be the impact? Jesus said, "*You are the salt* [spice] *of the earth...the light of the world. A city on a hill cannot be hidden. Neither do people light a lamp and put it under a bowl...let your light shine before men, that they may see your good deeds and praise your Father in heaven*" (Mt. 5:13-16). May our "salt and light" influence our government(s).

If those of us holding onto biblical Judeo-Christian principles bury our heads in the sand, and do not engage in our local and national political issues, then the least common denominator(s) will rule our lands. The vacuum will suck in unsavory people and philosophies. If we don't speak up, we will get what we deserve by our inaction. That being said, we must recognize several caveats about engaging in the process of government and politics: (1) We must recognize the difference between our personal political *opinions* and the written *Word* of God; (2) We should not operate out of the false *spirit of religion* that produces legalism and bondage. Sad to say, some people use the Bible as a menacing tool to attack their adversaries in anger. Rather, we should be engaging in prayer, voting, and advocacy in view of the freedom that we enjoy in Christ Jesus. We should be joyous "life givers" and should seek to be attractive to all men, women, and children by our actions and words. Let us be bearers of the truth, and truth spoken in love; and (3) If we take positions of authority in governmental offices, we must be mindful of the oaths that we are agreeing to uphold. Oaths are not to be entered lightly. It is better to not pledge, than to pledge and not pay. Don't take oaths, pledges, and covenants lightly.

God has prompted me toward intercession and declarations in relation to other nations' governments, beyond the United States. I had the privilege of preaching in Lagos, Nigeria during the Easter season of 2001. I was invited to Nigeria on behalf of Pastor Oyitso Brown of the Redeemed Christian Church of God (RCCG), via my friend Samuel Sorinmade, an RCCG pastor in Boston, Massachusetts. The RCCG is the largest denomination in Africa and is growing rapidly around the globe. Their General Overseer, E.A. Adeboye, holds the world's largest assemblies of mankind. At present, the RCCG draws millions (plural) of people at one time and place to their "Holy Ghost" prayer and worship services near Lagos.

It was an honor to be asked to speak at the National Gymnasium at their annual Easter music festival. While there, I wore my centurion's armor and spoke about spiritual warfare (see Eph. 6). I concluded by declaring a prophetic blessing over President Olesugun Obasanjo, a Christian leader who is attempting to root out the extreme corruption of their land (although he wasn't present at the meeting). Nigeria is a somewhat dangerous country, but a spiritual "sentinel" nation to the world. The Kingdom of God is advancing there in the face of great spiritual opposition, which in the natural realm is visible as the oppressive "spirit of religion." I have discerned some insights from the Holy Spirit about this key nation, and I anticipate ministering there again to large audiences. After I was there preaching, the Islamists in the North began to fervently attack Christians, killing many of them. We should keep our spiritual eyes on Africa and especially the nation of Nigeria, which is a *prophetic forerunner sentinel nation*. The Nigerian Christians are deserving of our attention and prayer. They model strength, courage, faith, and holiness to the Church of the world. They are also fighting a noble *spiritual* battle against the onslaught of the Global Islamic War that has been so devastating in Africa. God, I thank You for courageous Nigerian disciples of Jesus!

During the first visit to Nagpur, India in 2000, God planted a revelatory seed of faith within me concerning Sonia Gandhi's political future and the future government of India. She is the widow of Ragiv Gandhi, who was assassinated while serving as Prime Minister. I started intercession on her behalf in 2000. Then, in 2002 while preaching to thousands of people in India, I started making public prophetic declarations about her future that she would be elevated to lead the nation. Many witnesses recall those words spoken in India, the United States, and elsewhere. That destiny began to be realized during the "unexpected" miraculous upset in India's general election in May 2004 in which Sonia's Congress Party won. She could have chosen to serve as India's Prime Minister, but she deferred to her colleague. It was her decision, although heavy-handed Hindu nationalists were overwhelmingly berating and threatening her in the event that she would choose to become the PM. I am still praying for her key role in leading India and for that nation's destiny within the Kingdom of God. May God Almighty bless and anoint Sonia Gandhi in India, just as He did with Joseph in Egypt and Daniel in Babylon! May Sonia lead India with integrity and with the favor of God resting upon her.

Since the Bush administration started suggesting in the fall of 2001 that Iraq was a likely target for military action to attempt to avert more Islamist terrorist actions, I discerned on several occasions what would happen in the future of the Middle East region, and I shared those remarks in advance to others. For instance, in March 2002, one year before the war commenced, I experienced a very graphic dream/vision about being in a war in urban attacks by soldiers. I knew that war was inevitable, even while many people were praying that Saddam Hussein would peacefully go into exile. I also anticipated that it would be like a "war without end," and that the US and allied UK troops would need to "occupy the land indefinitely" for many years or decades, in spite of numerous comments to the contrary by the US governmental officials to the media. As a consequence, the occupying troops would encounter ongoing casualties and fatalities indefinitely. I also told friends about realignments that I believed would happen regarding allied air force bases and deployments in the Middle East, including key changes in Saudi Arabia, which serves as a fermenter, facilitator, and sympathizer of Islamic terrorists. Please note that the USA and its few allies aren't really engaged in a "War on Terrorism" *per se,* as it has been misleadingly termed in the media. Rather, the USA-led coalition has actually been fighting against the "Global Islamic War," but they don't choose to use the latter terminology in order to appear "politically correct" and culturally sensitive.

Coincidentally there were three other key developments that weighed very heavily on my heart: (1) The US State Department pushed hard diplomatically for a "Road Map to Peace" in Israel, that would force Israel to surrender land and to split up Jerusalem, thus providing key strategic concession to the Palestinians. Unfortunately the previous President, Bill Clinton, opened up that can of worms by his words of compromise near the end of his administration; and (2) I was led repeatedly to study the biblical borders of Israel, with an emphasis on the Euphrates River as the true northern and eastern border of biblical Israel, in spite of what our modern maps indicate to the contrary. These two issues further clarified in my spirit and mind that we are living in remarkable days. On one hand, American and allied (mostly British) troops occupied the land of the Euphrates. This river is crucial both naturally and spiritually! And (3), on the other hand, the so-called European allies frequently spoke anti-Semitic curses against Israel and Jewish people. This is a profound irony and ambivalence by the Western nations. America and other Western nations should not be schizoid and abandon God-honoring support for Israel (see Gen. 12). Any attempt to distance ourselves from the Jewish people and Israel will result in harm for the USA or any other nation who accepts anti-Semitic policies. *(However, it should also be noted that the modern nation of Israel, which has shown great military restraint toward the Palestinians and neighboring Islamic nations thus far, also has a responsibility to give proper consideration and treatment to their indigenous "occupants." Just because they are the Jewish nation of Israel does not exempt them from biblical compassion.)*

ALABAMA GOVERNMENT AND POLITICIANS

Concerning state governmental issues in Alabama, starting in 1996 God has been speaking to me about the poor and under-privileged through the Scriptures of the Hebrew prophets Isaiah, Jeremiah, and Zechariah, from ca. 700–500 BC. This same message of compassion was repeated by John the Baptist and Jesus in the first century AD. God Almighty is extremely concerned about our actions and compassion toward the widows, aliens, orphans, fatherless, poor, and the oppressed! I have been quite disturbed by the spiritual problems of the state of Alabama since establishing my home here in 1995.

Years ago I discerned that one of the major spiritual strongholds over this state is a lack of hope by the poor, the *spirit of hopelessness*. Over several years I've told many people, including some of the powerful businessmen and politicians in Alabama, that this state will move forward in its destiny of intended blessings only after we restore "hope for the poor" *verbatim*. Alabama is in the center of the "Bible Belt" of the southern USA, and as such, is greatly blessed with a rich Judeo-Christian heritage and a sizeable percentage of believers. But, the state also suffers from another spiritual stronghold, the *spirit of religion*, which is another major evil to contend within this state and the southeastern region. The spirit of religion is an obstacle to successfully fighting the spirit of hopelessness in Alabama. Coupled to these two strongholds in Alabama is a third ingredient identified by the prophet Bob Jones (of North Carolina), the *spirit of self-pity*. The enemy has a strategy of using multiple layers of demonic strongholds and principalities to enslave geographic regions. Alabama may be located in the heart of the Bible Belt with a high percentage of believers, but satan has been quite effective within this state. May God raise up powerful disciples to fight the strategies of the enemy within Alabama and elsewhere within the USA.

Then, in the Spring of 2001 I was in Washington DC in the office of Congressman Bob Riley. It was around this precise time that he announced (or was just about to announce) that he would run in the Republican primary for the state's highest office of governor. As I stood before him, the Holy Spirit revealed to me that if I declared it, he would become the next governor of the state. Immediately after receiving this revelation, I received a "check" in my spirit to not say anything at that time. In those times, Bob Riley, a very conservative, Republican congressman was considered to be a long shot with very poor odds of winning the Republican primary election or the subsequent general election against the incumbent Governor Don Siegelman.

Ironically, I had the privilege of subsequently praying in the State Capitol building in Montgomery while Siegelman still held the office. God was extending His grace to the incumbent for a season. Siegelman was graciously given time to change by the Lord. But, it appears that he did not change quickly enough.

It became clear within my spirit within several months prior to the general election that I was to declare that Riley would win. I declared this out loud and recorded it in my journal. Then, on the morning of the election, someone with a "supposed prophetic gift" phoned me immediately prior to my voting to declare in presumption and error saying, "The Lord told me that Governor Siegelman will win and by 'X' number of votes." To the contrary, I replied that that was not what I had sensed by the Holy Spirit's promptings, and that the issue was settled several months earlier. I replied, "Not only do I believe that Riley will win, but it will be the closest election in the history of the state's governor's race. It will even be hard to tell tomorrow who the winner is." Well, at the time immediately prior to the election, the opinion polls suggested that the incumbent Siegelman would win by several percentage points. However, in fact it was the closest race ever and the official results were not concluded for many weeks. Bob Riley was elected! Just as the election results for G.W. Bush in 2000 were contested in Florida for a period, a similar thing happened in this extremely close race for governor of Alabama.

Then in 2003, Governor Riley (who is a believer), and aided by a wonderful Christian man of high integrity, Drayton Nabers (then the head of finance for the state), proposed the largest tax and accountability changes in the history of the state, declaring publicly that it was about providing *"hope for the poor"* verbatim. He did so courageously, even though he was a staunch conservative Republican who had routinely fought against every federal tax he had encountered. The unpopular proposition failed by a 2:1 ratio. But, Governor Riley's courageous attempt served as a clarion call to everyone in this state to address the issues of taxation disparities that harm the less fortunate. May God set Alabama free from its evil spiritual strongholds (i.e., hopelessness, religion, and self-pity), provide hope for the poor, and move forward as the great "First State" of blessings to the Southeast region and nation. I believe that God has positioned me and other servants of the King of kings here for this critical time in the state's history.

INDIA AND CONFIRMED WORDS

In addition to the prophetic words concering Sonia Gandhi, I've experienced many *confirmations* regarding India. In recent years I have prayed that whenever I am invited to preach at a conference or church, that at least one individual will come forward to precisely confirm the message that I intend to deliver to that audience. It has become routine for the Holy Spirit to provide remarkable concordant confirmations within at least one individual who is attending. By the favor of the Lord, confirmations of teachings and prophetic words are very common in my life, and sometimes happen even multiple times within a single day.

My family became interested in Indian food and culture while living in London. I have a passion for the peoples of India, and I have faith that God will continue to use Path Clearer ministries to impact and "clear a path" for India for the Kingdom of God. So, it is a privilege to serve on the Board of Directors of Reaching Indians Ministries International (RIMI) within the USA and referred to as Mission India inside of India. RIMI is a frugal and productive mission organization that was founded by my good friend Saji Lukos, a hardworking man of faith. In February 2000, Saji and Moni Lukos visited me in my office to solicit my involvement with their exciting and growing early-stage ministry to the nation. I had just resigned in January from being the cofounder and president of a new ministry in Eldoret, Kenya. So, within minutes I enthusiastically agreed without any reservation to join the Board of RIMI. I have made many trips to India to preach, teach, and conduct Judeo-Christian leadership conferences.

On the first trip in 2000, while teaching the RIMI-affiliated Bible students in Nagpur in central India, I informed them at the start that I expected that they would witness many miraculous things themselves that week. At the end of the week approximately one dozen (one third) raised their hands when asked if it was true, and several offered testimonies of amazing things they had seen God perform through them that week. One day I was teaching them on the life of Joseph, the son of Jacob. In the midst of telling the life story of Joseph, I paused and directed 11 young men to come forward and line up in front of the class as a graphic analogy of Joseph's brothers. I quickly placed them in an ordered line and mentioned that they represented Jacob's sons from the oldest to the youngest. Pointing to the fellow at the end of the line, I said, "You are Benjamin." The students were in awe! Apparently I had, although unaware in the natural sense, in a few seconds, rank ordered the 11 by ages; and the last young man's actual name was Benjamin.

During the same teaching session at the Holy Spirit's prompting I delivered a message entirely out of context and without prior planning concerning Hebrews 10:19-39 and the need to persevere during difficulties. I declared to the Bible students to write in their Bibles, "This is for you. This is for India. This is for today." Then, they were exhorted to study that Scripture passage that evening. At an evening church service, a visiting pastor, whom I had not met, confirmed the same message and Bible passage *verbatim*. He felt that God had redirected his message away from what he had prepared during the prior days, and that he was diverted away from delivering his planned message. What joy it is to experience the revelation and power of God in operation, and to encourage these young ministers of the gospel.

In January 2003, I spoke at a large public meeting in tropical Kerala in the south of India at the invitation of my friend KC John, whom I had met the prior year while preaching in "his" local church (see "President Bush" previous). Before leaving, I had mentioned to the intercessors at home that I knew in my spirit that persecution was about to increase in India very soon and likely during January. I sensed that I must go to Kerala very quickly and before the anticipated possible war within Iraq, which started thereafter in March. I had believed that if I delayed going to India, I might not have the opportunity to speak at this meeting. KC John had indicated that I could either start or conclude the public meetings lasting for 21 days in Vellarada. Most preachers would naturally desire to speak at the conclusion when the audiences have grown considerably, in order to increase the numerical impact. But, God had indicated to me to start the meetings, when the audience was several thousand, but still much smaller than at the conclusion of the event.

While I was preaching in Vellarada for a couple of evenings, another foreign preacher was physically attacked in the capital city of Trivandrum. His arm was injured during an assault presumably carried out by xenophobic religious or political radicals. After my preaching only two nights, the regional governmental authorities blocked all subsequent foreign guests from speaking at large public meetings. Had I waited for the conclusion of the meeting I would have wasted a plane ticket for ca. $1,800 flying there and wouldn't have been permitted to speak at the public events.

Another fascinating "coincidence" happened on that trip. All the numerous e-mails to plan this trip's itinerary were either lost or not opened, in spite of numerous attempts by me to communicate to my coordinator. When I arrived in the capital city of Trivandrum, Mathews Lukos, who coordinated my itinerary, was hustling to establish a suitable schedule. Neither he nor I liked the frustrating chaotic situation. Yet, I knew I was to be there in Kerala at that precise time. Only the day prior had he obtained a governmental official's approval for me to speak in public, and an arrangement was made for me to stay in the home of a local pastor. Mathews hadn't met this pastor, who was located a short drive from the conference site. When Mathews and I arrived at this pastor's family home, I had been traveling for ca. 40 hours. I was tired, frustrated, and wanted a bath (using a bucket and a cup to dip the water), and to go lay down and take a nap.

After several minutes of chatting and looking at this pastor and his wife in their lounge, it was as if scales fell from my sleepy eyes. Voila! In the world's second largest nation of one billion people God had arranged for me to stay in the home of Pastor Tom Oothupan, whom I had met briefly and prayed a blessing over at my home church's first Missions Conference just one year before in Birmingham, Alabama. It was an amazing and highly improbable sign from God. Neither Pastor Tom nor I had planned this in advance. It just came together by the hand of God while I was on the jet plane riding to India, knowing that God desired to use me at that precise time. I experienced immediate joy and peace knowing that God can arrange anything as an "open door" for us in ministry. Jesus said, *"Nothing will be impossible for you"* (Mt. 17:20b), i.e., for His disciples who have real faith. Not only was it a pleasure to be reunited with a prior acquaintance, but Pastor Tom Oothupan then interpreted for me while I preached and taught in English at that conference many times. We were mutually blessed by one another. Thank you, El Elyon, for that encouragement at a critical time, when I was experiencing one of the most profound faith-testing seasons of my life. Meeting Tom also served as a catalyst for intercession within me toward the policies of the state government of Tamil Nadu, and favorable signs of change arrived in that state in May 2004.

I have taken preaching mission trips overseas in spite of facing stressful obstacles in my own business back home. I strive to live by the principle of *"seek first His kingdom and His righteousness"* (Mt. 6:33a). That means that obedience to the voice of God is #1. Following this, my wife is #2, my children are #3, my business/career is #4, and other home activities, hobbies, and avocations follow in priority. While on these trips, God has used the confirming words of other believers and various prophetic words to overwhelmingly demonstrate that He is a good God and Father to us. We are His precious sons and daughters. He knows our needs while overseas, and He knows our needs while at home. We need not worry about the difficulties we face while on mission trips or back home in our families or businesses. We need to be reminded of the words of Joshua (and Moses before him), *"...Be strong and courageous. Do not be terrified; do not be discouraged, for the Lord your God will be with you wherever you go"* (Josh. 1:9). This is perhaps my favorite verse in the Bible.

I have preached many times to a congregation of Keralite Indians at the International Christian Assemblies of God Church in Chicago, Illinois. Without fail each time I speak there, someone confirms the message I had planned in advance. Before the first visit, I personally had written notes about how the high school youth were facing spiritual warfare and that they needed to have the full armor of God (see Eph. 6). I had prayed for Holy Spirit confirmation in advance. A few minutes prior to being introduced to preach, Pastor Stephenson asked if anyone in attendance had a testimony to share. A man stood up and passionately reported how God had shown him that their "high school youth were in spiritual warfare and that they needed to use the full armor of God!" I had never met any of these dear people prior to that day. Since then, I've returned many times to preach in their church, and each time some confirmation happens. If you expect God to move on your behalf and you do not doubt in your heart that the mountain will move as you have declared, it will (see Mk. 11:22-25)! Having seen and heard confirmations of words so frequently, it is honestly easy for me to expect that they will continue in the days ahead. They are like a handy tool in a spiritual tool belt. Confirmations are like the fingerprint of the hand of the Holy Spirit, reinforcing the time-liness of a particular word or message.

In 2003 I was preaching on another Sunday morning in their church and delivered a warning for that congregation about their destiny that required action. As I concluded this difficult word for them I said, "This message is so important that you should all fast and pray for the next seven days." I had not planned that precise message or this ending before standing up, but the Holy Spirit devi-ated me while preaching onto the course He had arranged for that day. Not knowing if this tough word would result in me getting the proverbial left foot of fellowship, I went to my seat in tears with a sense of deep concern for my friends. Pastor Stephenson then rose and indicated that everyone was to fast that week. After the session ended, a man came up to me and said, "Tom, you are not going to believe this!" I replied, "Go ahead. I've already prayed for and expected a confirmation." He then explained how he had seen a dream the prior morning in which the very essence of the warning I was delivering was shown to him, too. He concluded by saying that in his dream he was warned by God that they were "to fast and pray for seven days" to be obedient to the Lord, or else the words of warning would take effect. I pray that my dear friends in Chicago will fully heed this word and move onto a new growth vision to fulfill their destiny.

Here's another example. Upon returning from the trip to Kerala in January 2003, I was invited by a friend to meet with him and provide a one-on-one report about my recent preaching trip in India. During our discussion, I declared a bold statement, "Someone needs to fill a 747 (a Boeing jet) with American believers and take them to India immediately!" My friend was astounded and asked, "How did you know that?" I replied that I didn't know, but I had just spoken it into being. I had never before heard of anyone using a huge 747 jet for ministry. He then informed me of his participation in a project to purchase a 747 for evangelism. I further explained to him how my son Isaac and I had sensed for a few years that God was in the business of liberating private jets for support of global ministry for the Kingdom of God. I've been known to remark, "Why should the best transportation and communication technologies only be available for those who serve the god of mammon in business, entertainment, and luxury? Shouldn't Judeo-Christian ministries also have access to the best technologies?" I desire for ministries of integrity and impact to have them available for key ministry needs.

A few weeks later I was a guest on board a leased *private* Boeing 737 jet flying back to India for several mission projects. While there I spoke again to a small church in New Bombay that meets in a high school, built by the charity of a local Christian businessman and influential politician, Mr. Pinto. On my prior visit at that high school-based congregation I had declared by faith to my hosts that I would soon meet that man. Then, on the very next trip only a month later I was on the stage at a large evangelistic meeting in Bombay. On the first night of the evangelistic meeting, a friendly Christian Indian woman warmly greeted me, which is unusual, as women in India seldom approach a man in public with such obvious confidence and warmth. I learned the following night from my colleague that she was coincidentally the wife of Mr. Pinto. She located her husband for me, and I spoke a blessing over them. Note that I had not sought them out, but God arranged my path to coincide with Mr. and Mrs. Pinto's plans, as per my faith declaration the prior month.

Here are a few other examples of timely confirmations. In the summer of 2003 I spoke on a Saturday and Sunday in Chicago immediately prior to KC John, and both times via the Holy Spirit's leading I anticipated the Scripture or principle that he had prepared and was about to deliver when he stood up to preach. One topic was regarding Jeremiah chapter 1 and the other topic was on Samuel anointing David prior to David using the five smooth stones to kill Goliath. On Sunday as I mentioned Samuel's anointing of David, KC John leaned over and remarked to Saji Lukos that I had just stolen another message from him. It was hilarious! Then, a couple weeks later in New York at the Pentecostal Youth Fellowship of America annual conference I mentioned briefly Elijah and Elisha. I declared that God is currently birthing a *prophetic nation of Elishas* among the youth and young adults under ca. 30 years of age. At the same time KC was in the auditorium adjacent to the one that I spoke within, and we both mentioned a similar topic without even meeting together. That made several confirmations between us. Holy Spirit, You are awesome. Your confirmations are encouraging!

God is doing a remarkable work in India in this season, as He is intent on transforming a nation! The youth of India will be *the* key to its development this decade. It is so exciting to be there in these days and watch Holy Spirit revelation in action essentially every day. If you doubt these examples really happened, you can find them and many other true evidences recorded in my journals, and in most cases there were abundant witnesses. Jehovah is a miracle-working God, who speaks to us in rhema revelation and desires for us to trust Him in real faith. He rewards us like a favored child when we do.

TUNING FORK SIGN

In July 2003, I was preaching at a Messianic Jewish CEASE (Christians Eradicating Anti-Semitism in the Earth) meeting in

Atlanta hosted by Jennifer Scrivner. I spoke about the need to correctly discern the false spiritual giftings and counterfeiters (i.e., false prophetic words, signs, and people) in our times of great outpouring of both good and bad spiritual powers. While doing so I mentioned, "The tuning fork of the Holy Spirit will resonate within us when we encounter someone else who is led by the Holy Spirit." As I said these words, the wall immediately behind me (a few feet away) make a perfect-pitched tuning fork sound for several seconds at a relatively low volume (like a whisper), but clearly audible to me! I smiled and looked behind me, and then asked, "Did anyone just hear anything?" Approximately eight to ten people quickly raised their hands. When asked what each of them had heard, in joy they replied that they heard a tuning fork coming out of the wall! Two ladies, who are musicians, knew the precise pitch. I suspect that for some of them it was one of the clearest *signs* from God they have ever witnessed. God was playing with us as His children!

These are the "days of Elijah"; definitely exciting times. The Holy Spirit was confirming the truth, relevance, and critical timing of the message that I was delivering, even though it was not the message I had prepared in advance for that evening. For many years, God has been faithful in routinely confirming in amazing ways the messages that He prompts me to preach. I have many true stories of confirmed words, and a few examples involving signs, as in this latter case.

SEPTEMBER 11, 2001

The tragic events of the attacks upon US soil by multiple Islamic warriors connected to Osama bin Laden and the Al Queda organization have been seared into our collective nightmarish memories. Many people have questioned, "How could God permit such a thing to happen?" They pondered whether someone knew some warning in advance, either in the physical or spiritual realms.

I don't know how many people around the world experienced these events from a perspective similar to me...while on my knees and prostrate on the floor in prayer. But, I definitely knew in my spirit that something very grave was about to happen prior to those events. I was drawn into an intense two weeks of prayer leading up to 9/11. I could barely get any work accomplished. I couldn't concentrate, as my thoughts turned exclusively to intercession. But, I wasn't sure what it was that needed prayer. On the weekend prior to 9/11, I had a phone conversation with my dear prophetic friend John Manwell in Liverpool and mentioned that something very serious was afoot. I asked for his impression. John shared a remarkable vision he had seen about skyscrapers falling from the sky, an accompanying earthquake, and a major stock market collapse. I asked him where, and he believed it was likely in London, where we both formerly lived. I was in agreement with him in my spirit overall, but I questioned whether the city was in fact London at that juncture. Although John did, I did not sense that London was in any imminent threat at that juncture. He had most of the prophetic understanding and I had a small piece.

Then, a few days later on the morning of September 11th I was sitting in my chair at home reading a pleasant passage in my Bible before going to work. Without any prior notice I instantaneously witnessed a trance briefly. The room disappeared and I clearly saw a large black flying winged object, like a large bird (or perhaps a plane) in form. It was flying directly into me at high velocity and would crash almost immediately. In shock I shouted out loud, "No!" and the trance disappeared. It lasted only several seconds. I sat there with my heart racing in my chest, not knowing exactly what this flying black bird message meant. However, I did know for sure that it involved the *angel of death* and that human lives were at risk. I began to meditate on the term *angel of death*. People were soon to die. Without knowing it, that was the precise time when the four commercial jet planes were beginning to be hijacked by suicidal Islamists in the eastern USA. Within a few short hours that morning, tragedy and chaos would hit the East Coast. The ground would tremble upon impact of the collapsing buildings and a stock market collapse would quickly follow…just as John Manwell and I together had foreseen in advance.

Shortly thereafter I was at my desk in my office at work, and an employee, Gayle Christopher, rushed in to say that a plane had just crashed into one of the World Trade Center buildings in New York City. She didn't know much about the details or if it was an accident or intentional. I discerned something immediately and told her specifically these words, *"Regardless of what you hear or see today from the media, know this for sure—it is about Israel and the Jewish people."* I quickly went into a position of prayer and intercession in tears while on my knees and prostrate on the floor in my office. Gayle and Teresa Packard joined in united prayer, and they are reliable witnesses of these events and answered prayers. I was praying out loud for revelation of information and for mercy for those affected people in New York.

I now know the meaning of that morning's vision of the black flying bird (or plane). The trance image has striking similarities to a Scripture from one of the Hebrew prophets, Habakkuk, *"I am raising up the Babylonians...**They fly like a vulture swooping to devour;** they all come bent on violence. Their hordes advance like a desert wind and gather prisoners like sand. They deride kings and scoff at rulers. **They laugh at all fortified cities...**"* (Hab. 1:6,8-10, emphasis added). Although this Scripture refers historically to events of the captivity of the Hebrews from Judea many centuries before Christ, I believe that this passage also is prophetically connected to the religious terrorist events of September 11, 2001. It should be mentioned that 2,500 years ago the Babylonians did not have military capabilities that involved flight "like a vulture." But, on 9/11 militant religious Islamists from the regions near ancient Babylon (the Middle East centered in Iraq) had come down like a vulture swooping to devour.

When the second plane crashed in New York, without hesitation I declared these words out loud, "God, ground all domestic flights **now!**" Within less than 20 minutes we heard a report that the US government had just grounded all domestic flights. When the third plane crashed into the Pentagon in Washington DC, without hesitation I declared these words out loud, "God, if there is a fourth hijacked plane, cause it to crash **now** missing its intended target!" We heard the report later that a fourth plane crashed into a remote field.

This was an amazing day! I believe that the two weeks of heavy intercessory prayer leading up to it had sensitized my spirit to discern the now rhema revelation of the Holy Spirit. Interspersed in the prayers about the hijackings were other prayers. For instance, I prayed about safety for the children of Muslims living in the USA. Then, I received a phone call from an Iraqi businessman living in the USA. I told this stranger that I had just prayed a blessing over him and his family. It really shocked him pleasantly, and he phoned me later that night to thank me for the consideration shown to him during a very stress-filled day of anxiety for his family and friends. In addition, I prayed for Jews living in New York City, and the phone rang from a Jewish businessman formerly from New York. I spoke a blessing over him and his family.

One final curious prayer happened during this extended time of prayer; I suddenly sensed something was wrong with my youngest son, Thomas. I prayed for him out loud and then turned to Gayle and declared to her, *"God wants to demonstrate to you now that He is speaking clearly!"* Having said that, within minutes the phone rang. Thomas' school was calling to say that there was a health concern with him, and could I please come to the school to pick him up. God was speaking clearly that day!

When the political rhetoric began in Washington DC to shift focus from Afghanistan to invading Iraq, I was not convinced that it was necessary and justified to proceed to full military engagement by the US and the UK in Iraq. In addition, I was very suspicious and concerned in my spirit of some of President Bush's appointed inner core advisors, including Vice President Cheney. I sensed that some of these advisors would not provide God-honoring counsel. However, I did know that war was inevitable. In March 2002, one year prior to the start of the war I had received a detailed graphic dream (or night-time vision) in which I was a witness to modern military fighting with infantry soldiers being deployed by helicopters into a poor urban setting under enemy fire. I just knew that the war in Iraq was a certainty. I also discerned several other issues related to the Middle East region and the effects that would be felt once the battles started. For instance, it was clear that American and allied soldiers would continue to suffer attacks, casualties, and fatalities on a consistent basis after the war was declared as over. This in fact happened.

BUSINESS WARNINGS

The prophetic warnings that John Manwell and I experienced around the events of 9/11, are not isolated events in our lives. On occasion I've discerned warnings about the leadership and philosophies of corporations and governments. Once I discern the warnings I typically inform other people, and thus make myself accountable.

In early January 2000 I issued a couple of e-mail warnings to close Christian friends and to secular businessmen about Bill Gates and Microsoft. I encouraged the businessmen, including non-Christian stockbrokers, to sell Microsoft immediately. Microsoft's stock was at a 12-year all-time high. The company's stock fell to approximately one third of its value within several months of this warning. At that time, my discernment of Bill Gates and Microsoft was very keen, even though I had never met the man or visited the company in Seattle. Within hours of issuing another warning to some friends during the night, I read the morning headlines that Gates had just stepped down as the CEO...a surprise to me. I pray that Bill Gates will repent and enter into a relationship with Jesus as Savior and King, and that Bill will discern how to become genuinely generous with his wealth in accordance with the righteous requirements of the King. A man's life does not consist of an abundance of his possessions. And, what does it profit a man to gain the whole world, and yet lose his eternal spirit?

The world's system of pursuing and worshiping wealth is *detestable* to God Almighty (see Lk. 16:14-15). The love of money is extremely disheartening to me! Our Western society has been greatly deceived by the adversary about the value of money. Unless channeled properly into the Kingdom of God, money has no eternal value. Yet, money is a great god to many if not most people, and especially in the Western World. They will do almost anything to obtain, preserve, and grow wealth. The love of money results in compromised ethics and values to the ultimate extent so that the *end justifies the means*. A Christian businessman friend once said to me (paraphrase), "People who love money serve their false god of mammon better than most Christians serve their true God." They will do almost anything for their *god*. I agree that this is a sad reality.

I suspect that a large percentage of self-declared "Christians" are no better than the rest. In Revelation 3:14-22 the Church of Laodicea was rebuked for the spiritually numbing effects of dependence on wealth. The Church in the Western World needs to heed this stern warning, because the majority of folks within the church today is *"wretched, pitiful, poor, blind, and naked"* (Rev. 3:17b). They think they are in fine standing, but in fact they are grossly missing the mark.

I've also perceived in advance concerns about the leadership and philosophies of other companies, for instance: (1) the huge accounting firm Arthur Anderson, which surprisingly failed within a couple of years of my perception that something was inherently wrong but cryptic within that firm; (2) the "Dot Com" internet over-valuations, of which I informed venture capitalists many months prior to the collapse that this was a house of cards and to get out at all costs as soon as possible. They were riding a greedy profit-taking cycle and seemed to disregard this advice; (3) the senior management of HealthSouth Corp. in Birmingham, who had deceived their share-holders by concealing billions of dollars of fraud. I had visited the company on a few occasions and had sensed something oppressive, prideful, and out of balance with its leadership; and (4) another pub-lic firm, with whom I shared some of a concern with one of their cofounders. I knew that *if* a certain action was taken, this firm would face a difficult three-year period. That firm then experienced a pre-cipitous drop in stock value and unanticipated challenges.

My perception of these firms prior to their periods of diffi-culty was based in part on revelation of information that I could not know in the natural sense and in part on discernment of some of the firm's activities and philosophies relative to biblical princi-ples of wisdom. I've even experienced individuals attempting to manipulate me to declare or write that a certain company (they were interested in promoting) would be successful in the future. I refuse to let others manipulate my words, for selfish manipulation is a root behavior of *witchcraft*. We shouldn't permit people to put words in our mouths, because we're accountable for all of them. A prophetic voice must be very careful about what is declared in either blessings or curses.

That being said, even prophetic individuals do not always discern things precisely as God desires. They make mistakes. There are times when some of "us" gets in the way. Our own desires, opinions, and knowledge can complicate the revelation that God wants revealed. I have especially noted that I have greater accuracy and precision in prayer and prophetic words, when they have nothing to do with my immediate family. There are less of *my* desires to get in the way of *His* will. However, let us strive to listen more clearly to the voice of the Lord. We must be careful in stating whether something is an impression from the Lord (rhema), an insight from Scripture (logos), or just our own opinion!

INTERCESSION PRIOR TO DEATHS

My teenage daughter Catherine came to me in tears on a Sunday and asked that I take her to pray over a man suffering with cancer in a Birmingham hospital. That man was Bob Caine, a Christian musician associated with Bill Gaither's ministry team. Catherine had never met him, but was led by the Holy Spirit to pray for him. On Tuesday I came home from work early and asked her if she wanted to go to the hospital. She was convinced that we should go on the following day. She said, "No Dad, tomorrow will be a better day." So, on Wednesday afternoon I picked her up. As we traveled on the highway toward the hospital I said to her, "I'm joining my faith with yours today. Just tell me, are we praying that Bob be healed or something else?" She replied that it was something else. Moments later I was led to pull off the highway at Liberty Park in Southeast Birmingham. She and I prayed together while standing on the grass. She spoke these words while in passionate prayer, "...*Go in peace and be freed from your suffering*" (Mk. 5:34). I noted the time on my watch.

146

One hour later we were in the intensive care unit of the hospital attempting to see Bob, whom I had seen once before while he was performing, but Catherine had never met him. The attending nurse was shocked and asked why we were there. I said our purpose was to pray for Bob as representatives of MountainTop Community Church, which we were affiliated with at the time. He then told us that Bob Caine had just died, and I asked him when. It was precisely one hour prior. I turned to Catherine and she had a wonderful countenance of joy and sadness interspersed with tears running down her cheeks. I said to her (paraphrase), "God used your faith and prayer today to be a blessing to release him." We then met with Bob's family and told the story to them, and called one of his close friends, Nora Gilchrest, from MountainTop Community Church to inform her.

On another occasion I was attending a Christian Believers United (CBU) conference with many "Messianic Jewish" believers in Ridgecrest, North Carolina. During a wonderful and intense time of worship in singing, I went forward in the evening and laid down prostrate before the stage for a long time in anguished intercession, primarily for the salvation of my family in Kansas. I clearly envisioned in my mind my sister Theresa's prior husband, Jim Kiefer, and their son. I knew that the Holy Spirit was moving in power as many people were singing, "Let the Fire Fall!" That is an extremely serious thing to declare, pray, or sing! When the fire of the Holy Spirit falls, unexpected and serious consequences can happen. Fire destroys obstacles and brings repentance. I knew that I was interceding for my extended family and especially noted a picture of Jim in my mind at that precise time. I remember praying that God's will would come, and with genuine fear of the Lord I expressed, "God, You may do whatever You desire in my extended family in Kansas *tonight.*"

Within one hour after that prayer my former brother-in-law, Jim Kiefer, was killed in a shocking and tragic alcohol-related automobile accident. In 1987 I had told him to his face that if he didn't take action to change his life, I expected that he would die in an alcohol-related auto accident. I pleaded with him to change his ways that night in 1987. May God continue to be gracious to

Jim's son, daughter, and mother, whom I love. May God's will for their lives be fulfilled.

At the start of September 2002 I discerned in my spirit that my brother, Dan, who had been in poor health, was soon to face a very critical challenge. I sensed that God said to me something resembling, "If Dan cannot eat, you cannot eat. You must fast for seven days. If you do not fast and intercede, he will certainly die soon, and you will share some responsibility for his fate." So, I fasted and prayed for Dan for a week. I did not tell my brother what I had done. I then went to Europe on a business trip. After returning I received a phone call saying that Dan had entered the hospital immediately following my departure for Europe. He told me that a few days after I had left for Europe he had come within seconds of dying. I prayed two particular things for him during my fast, and God had apparently answered. One of those prayers was that his health would be subsequently restored. Well, within one year he regained approximately 50 pounds and was in a vastly improved state of health.

Dear reader, if you doubt that the prayer of a *righteous* man or woman is effective, please don't waste your time arguing with me (see Jas. 5:16). It is too late to convince me otherwise. I've performed the *praying faith* experiment many times over many years, and it works! Try it yourself and you won't be disappointed. And, if you need to see greater "success," consider the level of your own righteousness. The lack of righteousness can impede your prayer life.

BLESSINGS DECLARED

I would like to share with you some brief examples of the power of spoken prophetic words of blessing. When my oldest child, Isaac, was born in 1982, I declared over him out loud the following words, "May you be honest, affectionate, and intelligent!" All of these characteristics abound in his life. He is an exemplary and wise Christian leader and role model of exceptional maturity. He reminds me of a God-honoring Solomon. One of the three traits, in particular, has been strikingly noticed already. With regard to intelligence, he was a *national* champion in mathematics in the

USA several years while at Vestavia Hills High School, at the individual and team levels. Not only did this blessing affect Isaac, but the anointed honey from the comb also dripped down onto our second child, Catherine. She, too, became a *national* champion in mathematics at the individual and team levels for several years. She's very talented academically, artistically, and for ministry. For that matter, all four of our children are highly favored by God.

At the beginning of each year I often start a fast of thanksgiving to the Lord. During these times, He often reveals to me a key *word* about the year ahead. As I have declared that word over many individuals' lives, I've seen remarkable things happen. For instance on January 1, 2002, the word that I heard was *breakthroughs* in prayers that had been or appeared blocked for a long time. A few days after I had recorded this, Chuck Pierce, the apostolic-prophetic leader of the US Strategic Prayer Network circulated online a message he had heard from God about the exact same word *breakthroughs* at the same time. Many exciting things happened in my family, ministry, and relationships with others during that season as I continued to exhort others with this encouraging word, *breakthroughs*. This message elevated their faith as well. I've had other Holy Spirit-inspired words at the beginnings of other years that defined the key principle God was desiring to teach me that particular year, including for instance: *More of Him and less of me, Give generously,* and *The eye of the needle of a hurricane.*

Let us learn to become "blessers" of others. Since our words have inherent power, we have the opportunity by our declarations to set the captives free, to make straight the paths of holiness, to bring healing and restoration, and to hasten the Lord's return. Either we can declare blessings with our opportunities today and receive an eternal reward, or we can be self-consumed and fail to bless others and miss out during eternity.

In conclusion, please don't try to come up with theological doctrinal arguments to explain that miracles, signs, and remarkable answered prayers don't happen today. You are wasting your time. It is far too late to convince me otherwise. And, please remind yourself that I'm a scientist trained to not believe in the miraculous or the unseen realm of faith. Scientists want evidence before they'll believe. Miracles, signs, wonders, healings, prophecies, and confirmed words happen today! Chris Hodges, the wise pastor of my current local church in Birmingham, the Church of the Highlands, repeats a phrase he learned from one of his friends, "A man with an experience is not at the mercy of a man with an argument!" I say a wholehearted "Amen" to that! Experiences impact our hearts, whereas knowledge impacts our minds. Validated testimonies of experiences are powerful and are not subject to the whims or opinions of the listener.

By His grace, this is not an exhaustive list. There are additional powerful testimonies recorded in my journals over the past several years, as they are becoming quite common. You have been provided with only a small portion of the testimonies that are the results of passionate *praying faith*. God Almighty deserves the credit for all of these testimonies. I was just the conduit He chose to use. He was the source of all power and revelation. He provided His faith within me. I was merely obedient to His promptings.

Isn't it amazing that God chooses to use saved individuals as His representatives in the world? Isn't it amazing that His power is revealed through our weaknesses? When we're in the place of dependence on God in *praying faith*, we are naturally weak, but spiritually strong. Isn't it amazing that He chooses to limit Himself in using us? It is similar to attempting to drain the vast ocean one cup at a time. The infinite displaced into the finite!

Chapter Eight

QUESTIONS

1. Which of the author's testimonies did you find most encouraging?

2. Which of the author's testimonies did you doubt or disbelieve, if any? If so, why?

4. Explain a testimony of something wonderful or miraculous that God has done for you or through you.

5. If you were lost on an inhabited island or locked in a foreign prison without a Bible, would you be able to list from memory 12 key biblical truths (e.g., foundational memory verses)? Would you be able to give a testimony of a transformed life by the power of God?

6. Do you exhibit the "fear of man" that prevents you from speaking boldly about Jesus?

7. Do you desire greater spiritual power and confidence in your life?

8. Do you have any friends who are prophetic individuals?

Chapter 8

PRESUMPTION AND HEARING FROM GOD

If anyone does not listen to My words that the prophet speaks in My name, I Myself will call him to account. But a prophet who presumes to speak in My name anything I have not commanded him to say, or a prophet who speaks in the name of other gods, must be put to death. You may say to yourselves, "How can we know when a message has not been spoken by the Lord?" If what a prophet proclaims in the name of the Lord does not take place or come true, that is a message the Lord has not spoken. That prophet has spoken presumptuously. Do not be afraid of him (Deuteronomy 18:19-22, emphasis added).

It is not good to have zeal without knowledge, nor to be hasty and miss the way (Proverbs 19:2).

Haven't we all experienced times where we acted in presumption thinking that God was behind us and our plans, when in fact we had it wrong? We ended up being embarrassed when it didn't happen as anticipated. It seems that many contemporary writings and teachings on the topic of faith deal with only apparent successes and exciting testimonies of faith, but seldom on the failures and bad results. God does not honor presumption, and as a result people who experience failures can frequently become disillusioned or have their beliefs shattered. And, at the opposite extreme, there are plenty of other contemporary writings and teachings on the issue of failures focusing on restoration and pastoral care, but seldom on the successes. They are written from two different perspectives. There is an apparent lack of balance in teachings between the successes (e.g., prosperity and answered prayer) and failures.

IMBALANCED PERSPECTIVES CONCERNING THE ABRAHAMIC COVENANT

Presumption plays a major role in many of the failures in our spiritual lives. But, before directly addressing presumption, we must first lay an effective foundation of understanding. There are plenty of books and sermons in the Western Church today that deal with "half" of the Abrahamic Covenant (see Gen. 17). Most Jews and Christians have some familiarity with this covenant made by El Shaddai to Abram (later Abraham) thousands of years ago before he entered the land of Canaan and after leaving Ur of the Chaldees on the Euphrates River (currently Iraq). In essence, God spoke into being the following truthful promise—that He will bless His sons and daughters who are the natural offspring (i.e., Jews) as a result of Abraham's faith, as well as the adopted offspring of Abraham via the "amended" New Covenant. The "adopted" sons and daughters are those Gentiles engrafted into the Hebrew line as believers through faith via the shed blood of Jesus on the cross (see Gal. 3:15-29; Rom. 11).

Although I am an advocate of declaring life-giving blessings frequently and whenever possible, I find that in some denominations of the Western Church, especially in the USA, there is an overemphasis on the personal benefits of God's covenant to mankind. Many of us in the Western World have a *what's in it for me* attitude toward church and God. Travels to other Third World nations can effectively change this narrow and "selfish" perspective quite quickly. The emotionally moving and unsettling book entitled *The Heavenly Man* by Brother Yun of China is a great example expounding this disparity. Brother Yun has suffered many years in prison under horrendous conditions of torture for his obedient risk-taking beliefs as an apostolic leader of the underground church of China. Watchman Nee is another fine example of a courageous leader from China. He knew the benefits of suffering for the sake of the gospel, including imprisonment and torture. In addition, consider the extreme costs for other leaders: Hudson Taylor—the first missionary to China; William Carey—the first missionary to India termed as the "father of modern missions"; D.L. Moody—the evangelist of Chicago; and George Whitefield—the great evangelist to the United States at the time of the American Revolution. Sometime in the future when in Paradise, I would really enjoy interviewing each of these great leaders, and I intend to by God's grace. May that which is declared bound on earth be established in Heaven (see Mt. 18:18). I want to meet and congratulate them on a job well done, although in Paradise all glory goes in only one direction, toward God.

By contrast our comfort-seeking Western "church-ianity" does not balance the "prosperity and abundant life message of *blessings*" with the responsibilities of living a life of obedience, righteousness, holiness to God, regardless of the personal costs, including persecution and the consequences of spiritual warfare. "*Shall we accept good from God, and not trouble* [also]?" (Job 2:10) God is far more concerned with our surrender and obedience, than He is with our comforts and happiness!

I speculate that when we arrive in the Great White Throne Judgment in the heavenlies, we will see for ourselves that those individuals who paid the greatest price personally in this life will be those closest to the Throne of the Almighty. I highly encourage you to read Rick Joyner's book entitled *The Final Quest*, as it portrays a wonderful vision of the Throne Room. Does not the Scripture say that overcoming martyrs are very close to the throne? Wouldn't we rather spend all of eternity in close proximity to the radiant Savior, than spend our short time here on Earth in comfort? There will be rank in Heaven...some will be close and some will be far away from the Throne. Any man, woman, or child would be a fool to choose the latter. I prefer to reign with Him rather than just barely make it into Paradise with a *get out of jail free card*! Please don't set your sights too low.

The Abrahamic covenant relationship in a nutshell means that we are part of the family of the God of Abram (Abraham), Isaac, and Jacob (later Israel), and each party in this spiritual family has a set of responsibilities. He will bless us, provided we keep Him as our top priority of life and obey His commands. This message is not only part of the Hebrew Bible (often referred to as the Old Testament), but was reinforced strongly in the New Testament as well (see Gal. 3 and 4). Jesus said that if we loved Him, we would *obey* Him; and God our Father (Abba) would love us too (see Jn. 14:21). So as believers, we must be *obedient*, not just having head knowledge. Few preachers these days in the Western church emphasize that we must be obedient. With biblical head knowledge alone, we have no "right" to expect the blessings of God through the covenant relationship of a spiritual family.

SOURCES OF INFORMATION INFLUENCING OUR LIVES

When considering declarations of faith in advance, one should consider the sources and basis for believing that something is or is not God's will. If it is God's will, then it is not presumption: if it is not God's will, then it is presumption to proceed. The sources and basis for a belief can come from many paths, only a subset of which are reliable and God-inspired information:

- The logos written Word of God in the Bible.

- Rhema word (revelation) of God via the Holy Spirit.

- Signs, wonders, and miracles.

- Interpretations of the Bible, revelation, and signs.

- Denominational doctrines of Judeo-Christianity theology.

- Personal opinions, preferences, desires, and envy.

- Outside influences and influencers:

    Church leaders, such as apostles, prophets, evangelists, pastors, teachers, etc.

    The media, such as TV, radio, printed materials, advertisements, etc.

    Governmental authorities.

    Family, friends, and other people.

    Educators and the educational system.

- Mental and physical illness, exhaustion, depression, weakness, enthusiasm, and flawed character.

- The "fear of man" (concern with what other people might think or do).

- False prophets, counterfeits, liars, and deceivers.

- Demonic influences.

Thus, with this diversity of potential sources of information impacting our beliefs, it is critical that we learn to hear clearly the voice of the Holy Spirit. Likely the two most critical steps in accomplishing that objective include developing the fear of the Lord and knowing the written Word of God (Bible) well. El Elyon is the sovereign omnipotent Creator of all things, and we must fear Him. We must also strive to grow in maturity in accurately handling His precious words that have been recorded for us. The power "concealed" in His written words in the Bible can become power in our minds, lips, pens, and computer keyboards.

As a result of maturing spiritually, it becomes increasingly easier to discern the *general will* of God in most situations. Primarily we learn the general will of God as He reveals it in the Bible. Therefore, we must be students of His written Word. In addition to Bible knowledge, He deposits understanding, wisdom, and discernment via the work of the Holy Spirit within us, as we grow in maturity learning from His recorded words. Our understanding of His written Word becomes our spiritual autopilot informing us to make wise decisions. If you lack discernment about the general will of God, first turn to the written Scriptures. All other forms of information or insight are subordinate to the logos written Word.

Discernment focuses on discriminating between what is *best* from what is merely *good* (see Phil. 1:9-10), and placing the correct emphasis and priority on the relevant portions of Scripture in a given situation. The written Word is always true...all of it. But, some passages are more relevant to a particular situation at a specific time. Discernment guides us in establishing which passages take priority in that particular context.

Furthermore, concerning discerning God's will for our lives, the author of *Experiencing God*, Henry Blackaby, provides an excellent teaching. Blackaby says that if we don't know God's will, then here's a valuable tip—find a mature disciple of Jesus who does know the will of God and has evidence of God's anointing upon them. Join with that person (or ministry team) and support him or her. In so doing, you will be engaged in assisting someone else who is more clearly hearing God's call. Follow him or her.

It is quite sad, but I have observed that many so-called believers place a lower priority on the written Word of God than they place on extraneous issues (even though many can be good things), such as denominations, doctrines, traditions, national patriotism, family influences, political affiliations, personal preferences, and opinions. This is not right! How will we face the God of all creation at the Great White Throne Judgment and attempt to defend (if possible) why we held anything in higher regard than our fear of the Lord and careful attention to His written Word? Our opinions will not matter in that day. Our preferences will not matter in that day. Our denominational doctrines will not matter in that day. In all likelihood we will be embarrassed at the numerous errors we have believed about God and the "church" throughout our lives.

Our God is both a God of *love* and *severity*. Unfortunately the latter attribute is seldom mentioned these days in the comfort-conscious Western World. We shall be held accountable for our actions and words, including every careless word we've ever spoken. Scrolls (books) shall be opened in that day in Heaven, and everything shall be revealed. We must be reminded of that reality. He is a good God who loves righteousness more than He loves mankind! (Meditate on that thought for a while). His Word shall be vindicated over time...it shall come to pass. His righteousness will be revealed, even to the very people who claim today that He is a "god of *only* love, who does not judge anyone." That is a lie. Their opinions about Him will not matter in that day. For every knee shall bow and every tongue confess that Jesus Christ (Yeshua the Messiah) is Lord (see Phil. 2:10-11). Every knee will bow and every mouth will confess, whether they want to or not. God is sovereign and He will not be mocked by anyone. If this strikes you as strong, please repent and change your ways today. You still have an opportunity. Jesus will forgive you of all wrongs and accept you as one of His own. He is merciful.

How are we to discern God's voice? Let's start on the negative…how not to hear His voice. If you chose to *not* walk in righteousness and holiness, you will not hear His voice. Bill Gothard teaches that *a person's morality dictates his or her theology*. If you are morally bankrupt, you will choose a convenient theology that let's you off the hook easily. Examples include agnosticism, or the universalist concept of a "god of *only* love, who does not judge anyone," or "love is god," or the Eastern "there are many paths to god" varieties, all of which are biblical heresies. If you make repetitive decisions that are not in accordance with obedience to the logos or rhema revelation you have received, then your conscience will grow dull and you will not hear from Him. Romans chapter 1 indicates that God will permit anyone to walk away from the Truth because of their obstinate rebellion.

Then how do you listen to His voice? *"I am the good shepherd; I know My sheep and My sheep know Me—just as the Father knows Me and I know the Father—and I lay down My life for the sheep"* (Jn. 10:14-15). Prayer is a key ingredient to discerning His voice. Have you trained your spiritual ears to hear from Him? Do you seek His counsel in the written Scriptures? Without proper understanding of Scripture, you easily fall into presumption.

There are plenty of examples of men and women in the Bible who presumed and failed to act out of faith. Abraham was promised a son though he and his wife, Sarah, were too old to be capable of becoming pregnant (see Gen. 17). While waiting on this to come to pass, impatience drove Sarah to request her obliging husband to impregnate their servant girl. In turn, the servant girl, Hagar, gave birth to the *son of presumption*, Ishmael, who then subsequently gave birth to the Arabs (see Gen. 16). Sarah later gave birth to the *son of promise,* Isaac, who gave birth to Jacob, the patriarch of the nation of Israel and eventually Jesus (Yeshua). God blessed Abraham for his faith as evidenced by his belief in action concerning the son of promise Isaac, which was accredited to him as righteousness (see Rom. 4:3). The son of presumption, though he was blessed by God (see Gen. 17:18-20), caused considerable difficulties for not only that generation but also for generations to follow (see Gen. 16:11-12; Gal. 4:21-31). God's desire was for Abraham and Sarah to simply trust and wait on God to act on their behalf. Presumption altered those plans. This is the difference between following God's preferred *A-plan* and His *B-plan.* When we obey His voice in a timely manner we're doing His *A-plan,* which results in the *son of promise* being fulfilled for our lives.

Another example—when the Hebrew peoples had settled the land of Canaan after Joshua led them back into the Promised Land, the Hebrews presumed and demanded that a king be appointed over them, even though it was not God's "A-plan." Their presumption gave rise to Saul as the first king, as the crowds were judging Saul by the eyes of sight in the natural realm (see 1 Sam. 8–10). God permits us to pursue our own plans, even if they are flawed. He does not force His will upon us; except once His patience meter has run out of time, then His wrath is displayed for the good of all nations to observe. In this particular case, God did not want the Hebrews to have a king like all other surrounding nations. He wanted them to walk by faith in Him alone as their king, so that He could demonstrate His power to provide and govern them. It didn't matter what the consensus or popular opinions held in that region. But, their obstinate presumption resulted in three kings: Saul—a bad king, David—a good king, and finally Solomon—initially a good king who later turned bad, before the kingdom was divided into Israel in the north and Judah in the south. God's plans are not usurped by man's presumptions, at least not indefinitely. With time, His sovereign will shall prevail. Although God is patient, He will not strive with mankind. He simply grants us the desires of our hearts for our own good, even if they are corrupt desires.

Don't be confused! The world is full of deception, and we all fall captive to it...some more than others. The path to righteous and holy living is a narrow path. Jesus said,

I am the way and the truth and the life. No one comes to the Father except through Me" (Jn. 14:6).

Enter through the narrow gate. For wide is the gate and broad is the road that leads to destruction, and many enter through it. But small is the gate and narrow the road that leads to life, and only a few find it (Mt. 7:13-14).

In your mind please envision a compass dial of 360 degrees. The *truth* revealed by the Bible is represented as due north. You are to walk straight toward it without deviating. But, the enemy of the Kingdom will whisper to you, "Please take one lie. Any lie will do.", as my friend Howard Morgan says. There are 359 degrees of lies to choose from. For many of us, some paths are easy to discern as blatantly wrong (e.g., the anti-Semitic actions of Hitler's regime during the 1930's and 40's that forced the deaths of millions of Jews), but some are quite close to the truth and come very close to due north (e.g., an incorrect doctrine based on a flawed interpretation of a biblical passage). You can go a few degrees off of due north, feeling that you are heading toward God, yet you'll never reach the target.

Satan doesn't care how he misleads you. He's just concerned that he is ultimately successful at misleading you. The father of lies is willing to set you up with a "minor" lie containing a grain of truth, so that he can ultimately mislead you with a bucket of lies in sequential manner. Then, once you've taken that misstep, he piles on more lies like the multiple layers of an onion. Once "completed," a *worldview* based on six or more layers of lies is very difficult to turn around. Our enemy is *the* deceiver, *the* father of lies, and *the* author of the principle of the slippery slope. He hates you and wants you to be deceived concerning all truths. The power of deception is greatest when an individual is entirely unaware that he is deceived. The adversary is using this tool effectively on all of us, even church-attending Judeo-Christian believers. Deception is rampant within the world and within the "church."

OUR GREATEST STRENGTHS
ARE OUR GREATEST WEAKNESSES

Deception is easily accomplished when it plays into our areas of personal strengths. It is well worth noting that *our greatest strengths are our greatest weaknesses*. If we are naturally talented as an intellectual, then our minds are easily misled away from the King of kings by knowledge, education, and intellectual pursuits. If we are naturally talented with a beautiful or powerful physical body, then we are easily misled to place a vain overemphasis on the physical body. If we are naturally gifted and talented as a compassionate, merciful individual, then we are also prone to not discern or judge well the motives of manipulative individuals; they play upon our strength as a compassionate person and turn it into a weakness. If we are naturally confident in our minds, we are easily misled into pride, which is offensive to God. If we are naturally talented as an analytical, cautious, and prudent assessor of risks, then we are also likely to have great difficulty in exercising faith (risk-taking belief in action). If we are naturally talented as a creative musician or artist, we might also have greater difficulty using our craft to bring forth genuine "worship" to the Lord, as opposed to a technical musical or artistic "performance." These various examples are not an exhaustive list, but rather demonstrate the tendency for us to rely on our own natural abilities and capabilities in a presumptive mode or pattern. That which comes naturally to you as God-given inherent talent is often the enemy of spiritual growth and genuine faith.

It is important to note that this principle has implications not only for inherent natural talents, but also for our spiritual gifts, some of which are supernatural and operate in the miraculous realm (see 1 Cor. 12; 1 Cor. 14; Eph. 4). Natural talents and spiritual gifts are not necessarily the same thing! That may be a surprise to many of you, as even many well-intentioned ministers of the gospel do not know this. Some spiritual gifts are quite supernatural and miraculous in nature. I have noted a progression from talents to spiritual gifts to mature character. My friend Howard Morgan often teaches that, "Our *giftings* will take us where our *character* cannot keep us." I have added a further principle to Howard's solid teaching, "Our *talents* will hold us back from where the *giftings* desire to take us." Spiritual gifts are granted for use in the Kingdom of God for His glory and for the benefit of other people, for the equipping and building up of the Saints (see Eph. 2, 4). By design, the manifestations of spiritual gifts often reach beyond our present level of maturity in character. Thus, the spiritual gifts granted by God present us with tests to build up our character, while at the same time they are intended primarily for service for the benefit of others.

But, God is far more interested in our character than He is in our natural talents or our spiritual gifts. Thus, He instructs us to judge the character of other individuals based on the *fruit* of the Holy Spirit (see Gal. 5:22) evident within them, not on their apparent talents or gifts *per se*. Spiritual gifts can be easily counterfeited and can result in deception. There are plenty of counterfeits, pretenders, and pseudo-believers in the Church and elsewhere in the world. As we examine others for virtuous fruit (e.g., love, joy, peace, etc.), we are filtering the input information based on fruit as the top priority, not talents or gifts. However, the carnal individual will frequently look toward the talents and gifts, rather than the fruit of the Holy Spirit.

For instance, one might observe that a well-known evangelist is highly successful based on the high number of people attending or responding to a public message or the extent of TV and media coverage. Yet, the evangelist with the spiritual gift for evangelism might not be very mature. For instance, he might demonstrate overt pride, haughty arrogance, dishonesty and deception, manipulation, and lack of integrity. Yet, the gift can still operate even when his life is not properly aligned with the will of God in obedience. These "gifted" folks with poor character can be quite dangerous, and I know this from first hand experiences. We need fewer of them as ministers of the Gospel. We should pay careful attention to not be deceived by those who seem to have anointed giftings, yet the fruit of their own lives shows them to lack maturity of character. Many people have noted with disgust the hypocrisy of some televangelists who have overt patterns of sin, such as a proud spirit, an independent will, or an unbridled immoral pattern of life. However, let us follow those leaders who have not only anointed giftings and callings, but who also have walked the narrow path of righteousness resulting in solid character! Place the emphasis on their character, because that is how God will also be viewing them. He trusts those who have righteous character, not those who just produce some ministry results.

Chapter Eight

QUESTIONS

1. God makes each of us as unique individuals. How does God "speak" to you personally?

2. Rhema revelation is *always* subordinate to the logos written Word of God. Do you carefully check in the Bible for confirmations of the perceived promptings of the Holy Spirit?

3. In what ways have you erred in presumption in your life? How costly were those mistakes?

4. Have you been embarrassed by taking steps of faith or expressed prayers?

5. How much time do you spend listening each week to television, radio, conversations with unrighteous people, or via printed media? What influence are these forms of communication having on your own righteousness and holiness?

6. Hearing clearly from Jesus is dependent on knowing Him. What are you doing to know Jesus better?

7. The spiritual gifts of discernment and wisdom help prevent presumption. Do you have any close friends who have these invaluable spiritual gifts?

8. Define the differences between natural talents, spiritual gifts, and character. Which of these three demonstrates most clearly the *fruit* of the Spirit?

Chapter 9

DISAPPOINTMENTS AND DELAYS

Hope deferred makes the heart sick, but a longing fulfilled is a tree of life (Proverbs 13:12).

Let's turn our attention to disappointments or frustrations in a faith walk. Haven't we all experienced disappointments when we thought we were acting in accordance to the will of God, but we were only partially enlightened and misunderstood what He was trying to say or do? Haven't we all experienced delays while we have been waiting on God to "show up at the party" to answer our prayers and desires? What about taking risk, working hard, and still failing in spite of a hard effort to trust Him? A so-called "failure" in faith can serve to either make us better or make us bitter.

Most of the time in my life, career, and family I have received great blessings and favor by God. I've seldom experienced "failures." Sure, I've had some disappointments, delays, and frustrations in timing, but overall things have gone well in my life. I believe that this is due to His grace and favor shown to me coupled with my willingness to be obedient as He has directed. However, I would like to share a key example with you of a major disappointment from my own life.

On April 17, 1987 my youngest brother Pat, a 20-year-old premedical student at the University of Kansas, died in an auto accident while driving home from college. I deeply loved my brother, as did everyone in my family. At that time I was a post-doctoral research fellow at the Imperial Cancer Research Fund in London. I received a rare and extremely difficult phone call from my dad on Saturday morning, the 18th in London. When I heard my dad's voice, I immediately replied, "Oh no! What's happened, Dad!?" He said, "We're only going to have one doctor in our family." I exclaimed, "What happened to Pat!?" In my father's intense grief and shock, he said a brief remark (paraphrase), "He died in a car accident." He immediately hung up after saying only two sentences to me.

Just hours before Dad had been awakened during the night by the police. They delivered the dreaded report of the loss of his youngest son, to whom he was very close emotionally. This big strong man could barely speak. I then had to process this tragic, shocking, brief report while in London thousands of miles away from Kansas. I quickly arranged to travel for nearly 24 hours on a series of flights to get home. It was horrible!

It is hard to articulate how painful and disappointing this event was. The death and funeral of my brother was the single hardest event of my life to date. I loved him and had begun to invest spiritually in his life as a young believer of Jesus at the age of ca. 11. He desired to become a physician, and he had such a tender caring heart for everyone. He was very bright and a talented piano player. My family recalls a pudgy, content, intelligent, and cheerful boy learning to play "The 12th Street Rag" on the piano, as he was financially incented by our dad to master that song. The sense of loss was indescribable for my mom and dad, siblings, and me. Pat held great potential both professionally and for service to the Lord. But, that potential was cut short at the age of 20. It was a major disappointment and discouragement in our collective lives.

However, I have learned from this incident that God uses adversity to build character within us. We've heard it said that troubles make us either better or bitter. The pain of the loss of my brother has resulted in a positive impact in my life. His untimely death gave me a desire to reach out to even more people with the saving knowledge of Jesus. During the dark months following this tragedy, the Holy Spirit began a very deep and new work of revelation in my life. I was hearing more clearly from Him than ever before. It was at that "low" time that I heard God's calling, via a series of remarkable spiritual dreams. I would become involved in itinerant preaching while living in London. It was at that time that God began revealing his miracle-working power of the Holy Spirit around me for the first time. I am so thankful for our wonderful Bible study group at 66 Walpole Road in London. They were helpful to me during this grieving phase. Our valley experiences can drive us close into His loving arms and toward our destinies. Sometimes the great difficulties are manifestations of the gracious hand of God that nudges us toward new and better things. Let us rejoice that He uses those days of testing to refine us from impurities.

The Scriptures have provided us with many character sketches of God-honoring children and adults who encountered disappointments repetitively. Joseph and Moses both encountered numerous difficulties at the hands of the Egyptians, and perhaps even more disappointing to Joseph was the excessive, envious, and malicious treatment he received from his older half-brothers. Daniel encountered numerous difficulties at the hands of the Babylonians and Medo-Persians. And, Jesus encountered numerous difficulties at the hands of the religious Jewish leaders of Judea and finally the Roman oppressors. But, there is reason to be joyful and optimistic. Because Jesus endured difficulties and disappointments for our benefit, He can relate to the pains we encounter. He is a loving High Priest who intercedes for us at all times, including in our times of disappointments.

Next, let us consider a faith declaration or goal that fails to materialize because we incorrectly discern the timing of God's intentions. In 1997 and 1998 I began to experience promptings from the Holy Spirit that He was about to unleash some ministry and business blessings in my life, unparalleled in the prior two decades. The results of those revelations have since begun to be realized in my life, as this book bears witness. However, in particular a concept or "vision" of a headquarters and retreat center was developing within my son, Isaac, and me. This center would serve as the ministry headquarters and would host Judeo-Christian retreats. The concept and "vision" became clearer in our minds over the next several years. Since 1998, my son and I had been praying over land adjacent to the Cahaba River near Liberty Park, which is part of Vestavia Hills, Alabama.

Then, in the summer of 2002 Isaac became aware of an already developed property in that area that *appeared* to be what we were envisioning, and several coincidences were noted: (1) It included an already established conference center; (2) It was immediately across the narrow river from where we had prayed on occasion for many years; (3) I had a vision-concept sketch drawn of the desired facility in the front of my Bible prior to seeing this property. The sketch had a resemblance to the two-story facade of the main building, including six Roman columns; (4) It was now on the market and could be purchased possibly more affordably than starting a brand-new project on another piece of land; (5) Negotiations to sell one of my companies had provided early indications that an acquisition might occur; and (6) Several of my close prayer partners were consulted. They, too, agreed that it was likely a prompting of the Holy Spirit, and that we should proceed in our faith journey.

Without one percent of the necessary funds available, I obtained a contract to purchase the property, incurring a multimillion-dollar obligation due upon closing. I assure you this was one of the greatest steps of faith I had ever attempted to date...a proverbial leap of faith. It caused my heart to race almost every night as I pondered and prayed for God to reward this act of faith and provide sufficient funding for the project by October, when the contract was to close. I didn't have any extra money, as my two businesses were still in the early stages of development. So, I sought help from mortgage companies and investors.

But, the mortgage money never materialized on time and the contract lapsed, with me losing more than $3,000 on the property survey and quite a few hours of sleep. This was in large part due to the economic crisis subsequent to the tragedies of September 11, 2001. No commercial loans were bankable following the World Trade Center crisis. I had believed and trusted, and yet it did not come to pass as we had hoped and prayed. This was either *presumption*, which I doubt, or a major *disappointment*. Well, at least in part it was a major disappointment, and likely a God-ordained *delay* to test our faith. It was definitely a major test.

So, what are some of the lessons that I learned from this "failed" faith test? In summary: (1) The vision and desire was given by God to test us and grow our faith. In essence, were we willing to persist in spite of great obstacles?; (2) Spiritual warfare is very real. When you attempt great things for God, as the *Father of Modern Missions* William Carey exhorted us nearly 200 years ago, you can expect that the enemy of the Kingdom is going to pull out all the stops to postpone, stop, or interfere with your God-honoring plans. We need to not only know the good plans God has for us, but that the devil has serious plans and strategies to mess with our destiny. We therefore must solicit intercessors to partner with us during the warfare; (3) We "*know in part and we prophecy in part"* (1 Cor. 13:9). We sometimes miss God's precise intended meaning and timing. This is often related to our inexperience and/or incorrect level of enthusiasm for a desired outcome. Depending on our personality, we tend to act in obedience either too hastily or too cautiously. God is effective at messing with our natural emotional tendencies. If we depend on the Holy Spirit's leading we should be able to get the message and the timing correct; (4) I may have presumed that monies or obligations would be easier to obtain from certain sources than I realized; (5) Many months thereafter, I received a reproof from a man who stated that I had earlier spoken a "false prophecy" about our intentions to purchase the property, because the events didn't unfold as anticipated at that juncture. To him, it didn't matter that this change in my faith journey was largely due to the difficult financial climate immediately following September 11th. This dramatic change in circumstances for the worse prevented us from obtaining the necessary funds. I strived to respond graciously in truth to his remarks. First, the loss of the property and then the criticisms were disappointing and humbling situations to deal with back-to-back. Both disappointments happened in spite of the fact that we believed that we had not acted inappropriately in faith concerning the property. We can act in faith, and still we might be criticized, and especially so if the accuser considers our faith statement as a prophetic word. Often the criticisms come from well-intentioned individuals, who think they are trying to "help us," when in fact they might not fully understand all the circumstances or the intended tests that God is taking us through. I would rather experience a "failure" at a genuine Holy Spirit-prompted faith test, than fail to act upon risk-taking belief. Finally, (6) *"It ain't over till the fat lady sings!"*

I remain confident that God is moving us in faith toward developing a project of this type, perhaps either on that property on or near the Cahaba River, or another piece of real estate, or via some other process yet to be revealed (i.e., in "virtual" mode without a land purchase). If Jesus tarries long, we still hope to see this project established through Path Clearer ministries. A genuine faith statement is not dead until we give up acting in accordance with our belief. Though we may face a deviation or detour along the journey, we're still pursuing the target as best we understand the goal. Momentary disappointments should not deter us. We believe that it will happen, unless God redirects us to an even greater opportunity as a more favorable diversion. He may do as He wills. He may act when He sees fit. Perhaps someone might be led by the Holy Spirit to *give* Path Clearer ministries the land or facilities for a conference center.

I've been heartened to read of the outstanding biographical testimonies of faith of Rees Howells and George Mueller, both having formerly lived in the United Kingdom. These two spiritual giants moved mountains by faith through intercessory prayer. However, each has provided several examples of how the Holy Spirit directed them in genuine faith, yet pulled the plug on the course they had their hearts set upon, and then redirected them toward an alternative path. They even have specific examples about pursuing property purchases for their ministries by genuine faith, that didn't literally come true as they had envisioned and had been prompted by the Holy Spirit to action. But, God did fulfill the vision in some form…and in each case it was a glorious outcome. I highly recommend that you read the biographies of these two men of great faith. Let us not grow faint in believing the vision, for faith can adapt to changing circumstances as God progressively reveals more information to us about His will.

Remember, *"It ain't over till the fat lady sings."* Waiting is often the hardest part to faith. Persistence is a virtue. Consider the long list of outstanding testimonies of saints listed in the "Hall of Fame of Faith" in Hebrews 11. *"All these people were still living by faith when they died.* **They did not receive the things promised;** *they only saw them and welcomed them from a distance. And they admitted that they were aliens and strangers on earth"* (Heb. 11:13, emphasis added). They were living in faith and yet they never received what they were hoping for. They died before the fulfillment of their desires. The ancient prophets also frequently wrote prophetically of future events that were to happen long after their short lives were over.

If there is one area of discernment where we often fail, it is with the issue of the appointed *time* of fulfillment for a faith result or a prophetic word. We can easily miss God's calendar and appointed times in true prophetic messages. I have experienced many revelations of future events in dreams, but the timing of when these events are to occur is usually obscured. From my assessment the events are likely to happen, but the timing is not revealed. On occasion I will sense within the dream or upon interpretation that it is "very soon," but typically the timing isn't revealed within these revelatory dreams. I've had many experiences where the dreams came true the following day, but this is not the general pattern. The timing is often nebulous. Thus, we should be careful about stating a precise time for a future event, unless the Holy Spirit has clearly revealed that detail to us.

One final thought concerning the "failed" property purchase. In the summer of 2001 I had invited a Christian man to visit the property when it was under contract. During the visit he "kept his powder dry" about his own plans to do a somewhat similar project in his hometown. In 2002 I subsequently toured his elegant facility. It was like walking into a dream that I had envisioned before. I then recognized that even our statements of faith in the face of risks can have an impact on someone else's vision and actions. Our faith actions can be a stimulus, or confirmation, or can provide some insights about what another person might do or might do better. In addition, I've begun to strategize with friends about birthing a Path Clearer conference center near Birmingham and in other locations around the globe. It isn't about ownership. It is about God's desires being realized through someone or groups who are available.

While managing my two businesses I have had many restless nights of struggling in prayer and faith. I've experienced being awakened in the middle of the night in cold sweats on many occasions due to the various sources of pressures. The issues of raising sufficient investments, awaiting revenues, negotiating contracts, reducing staff, and attempting to sell a company can generate immobilizing fears. During these difficulties we must persist in warring prayer and most ironically peace in the midst of the storm (see Ex. 14:13-14). The enemy tries to discourage us innumerable times each day for weeks, months, and perhaps years. Yet, we should persist in genuine faith in the sovereign Lord, because God has a great destiny ahead for us in ministry and professional life.

We read in First Samuel about David's many struggles and how he had to persist time and again! Saul would pursue and attempt to attack David. But, after being gently reproved by David, Saul would seemingly "get it" and show signs of repentance. Presumably David was temporarily pleased at the outcome on many occasions, exhibiting his "love believes the best" attitude. However, then in the next scene,

Saul would be after him again. It seemed hopeless and very disappointing from David's perspective. It just happened over and over—David was like an innocent dog that was being hunted down. He was the outnumbered underdog without much power in the natural realm; his power was primarily in the spiritual realm of faith.

Through this process of testing, David and his men were being trained in persistence and courage. David was being trained as a king as well and as an intercessor for his team in great need. Just examine some of his intense cries for help in Psalms 13, 20, 77, and 90. Those numerous tests were used to make him dependent on God and not on his own natural abilities. God's destiny for David as king would be revealed in time, in spite of continuous skirmishes, battles, and Saul's actions that brought disappointments repeatedly into David's life. Those difficult and disappointing tests proved David's character and trust in God Almighty. David was trained over time to increase his level of faith. May we learn similar lessons and be pleasing to the Lord. David was anointed for the great purposes and extreme tests set before him. Remember that salvation is free, but the anointing will cost you your life.

Sometimes when we experience the "valley" of suffering, persecution, failure, disappointments, and delays, we are there not because we have sinned, but because we have *not* sinned—we are living righteously. Please carefully consider Uriah the Hittite and his wife, Bathsheba, at the hands of temporarily selfish King David (see 2 Sam. 11). Uriah was conveniently murdered on the battlefield by *David's actions*, Bathsheba was drawn into adultery by *David's actions*, and her son died as a result of *David's actions*. Had this married couple, Uriah and Bathsheba, deserved the treatment they received, just so that our sovereign God could refine the character of the anointed King David in the fire? There is no explicit mention in Scripture that either Uriah or Bathsheba voluntarily sinned, so the burden of culpability falls squarely upon King David for his irresponsible and selfish actions.

If we are living righteously, our suffering is often not retribution for a wrong done, rather it is God's will to permit us to be tested while we are doing what is right. When we arrive in that valley, we sometimes receive criticism and rebukes from others who don't have the *whole counsel* of the Lord. There is a major part of "righteous suffering," like Uriah, or Job, or Joseph experienced, that cannot be easily rationalized scripturally or using well-intentioned advice. On many occasions I have experienced some undeserved betrayal in my life, and it appears that it is often motivated by the other party's envy. Not to say that I haven't sinned plenty or haven't given cause for offense often, but I've been on the receiving end of unreasonable criticism many times. *"If someone asks him, 'What are these wounds on your body?' he will answer, 'The wounds I was given at the house of my friends' "* (Zech. 13:6). God permits accusations against us to benefit us as well as the party making the accusation. If there is truth to the accusation, then we must agree, repent, and realign our attitude. If there is little or no truth to the accusation, then our character is tested by our choice of response to false accusation. Jesus and the apostle Paul both endured many false accusations; they serve as our examples to emulate.

When a righteous individual is in a valley of undeserved pain and especially for a long season, what he or she really needs is a hand of fellowship that will encourage him or her. At that juncture, he or she doesn't need criticism or well-intentioned reproof. Please keep this in mind. We shouldn't kick a dog while he is down, and especially if he has done nothing (or little) to deserve punishment. The Book of First Peter (and also Second Corinthians) addresses the issue of righteous suffering. *"But even if you should **suffer** for what is right, you are blessed..."* (1 Pet. 3:14, emphasis added). *"And the God of all grace, who called you to His eternal glory in Christ, after you have **suffered** a little while, will Himself restore you and make you strong, firm and steadfast"* (1 Pet. 5:10, emphasis added). Persistence during righteous suffering can serve as a ramp onto a new plane of faith... from one level to the next. Suffering can transform *our* faith into *His* faith within us.

With regard to seeming *failures*, let us note once again that God is more concerned about our character being transformed than He is with the outcome of a single issue, win or lose. God uses disappointments to humble and guide us along the journey He desires for us. The path is not always straight, but often has surprising twists, turns, and deviations from what we perceived was "the plan." Even if we seem to fail at that moment, be encouraged by the poem of George L. Scarborough entitled "To the Men Who Lose," containing these lines:

> *Here's to the men who lose!*
> *It is the vanquished's praises that I sing.*

175

And this is the toast I choose:
"A hard-fought failure is a noble thing!
Here's to the men who lose!"
(emphasis added)

I have observed that many Charismatic and Pentecostal believers in the Western World in particular have a difficult time reconciling the biblical role of suffering and disappointments that is necessary to mature believers. Our greatest growth happens while we're tested "in the fires" of adversity. We should view apparent failures as just part of the *good* process that God desires to work in our lives. We shouldn't give up because of one failure or defeat. One profound example of enduring repeated failure is the life of 19th century US President, Abraham Lincoln. The scorecard for his political career was littered by innumerable disappointments, yet he became one of the most powerful men on Earth and was posthumously regarded as one of the greatest leaders of that century. His persistence and courageous actions helped preserve an entire nation at a moment of great cataclysmic tension.

It is worth noting that I have observed that disciples who earnestly desire to know Jesus intimately seem to encounter intense seasons of testing. When they get serious with Him, He in turn gets serious with them. Yet, they persevere and remain righteous in spite of the intense hardship. Some of them seem to be hit very hard even though they are seemingly doing everything right according to His will. It is as if God Himself punches His own servants down for their own good. You only need to study the life of *one* of His chosen prophets (whom He refers to tenderly as *"My servants"*) in the Hebrew Scriptures to see this clearly demonstrated. These prophets loved El Shaddai and volunteered for duty as one of His trusted servants, and voila, they're attacked or mistreated! The tests help us to identify with the sufferings of Jesus on the Cross of Calvary. Our response to those God-imposed tests releases His power and His faith within us. If you want to go through a deep test of your faith, just voluntarily pray "not *my* will, but *Your* will be done," just as Jesus yielded up to the Father's will. The adverse circumstances we endure should make us better and drive us closer to our sustaining God, El Shaddai. That is provided we don't give up. May the tests of adversity drive us from faith to faith...from dependence on our faith to dependence on *His* faith!

Chapter Nine

QUESTIONS

1. What have been the most disappointing events of your life? Why did they happen?

2. Have you prayed expecting something *big* to happen, but it did not? Did it leave you in a state of hopelessness or depression?

3. Consider the faith of Abraham. Would you be willing to go at the voice of God's command, not knowing where you were heading (see Heb. 11:8)? Would you be willing to give up your promised son, Isaac?

4. What is the longest you've had to wait for a prayer to be answered?

5. What have been the character-building lessons you have learned through difficulties, while waiting on God to reveal His answer to prayers?

6. How have the faith tests you've encountered resembled the tests that Jesus endured?

Part III

◆

Understanding the Kingdom

Chapter 10

THE KINGDOM OF GOD VS. THE "CHURCH"

Jesus said, "My kingdom is not of this world...My kingdom is from another place" (John 18:36).

First and foremost, the Kingdom of God and "Christianity" are *not* the same thing! The Kingdom of God and the "local church," at least as we commonly experience most local churches today, are not synonymous! These are shocking revelations to many Christians.

In order to have a proper understanding of the role of genuine faith in our contemporary lives, we should appreciate that Jesus preached extensively about the *Kingdom of God* (or *Kingdom of Heaven*, as Matthew commonly referred to it). At that time, these teachings of Christ were in contradiction to many of the teachings of the *religion* of Judaism, built upon the Mosaic Law of the Torah plus manmade traditions, many of which were of dubious value.

The Kingdom of God is quite difficult to summarize in a concise **creed** or *confession of faith,* as if because you simply believe or fulfill a list of criteria you're in the club. The concepts of the Kingdom are impossible to understand using merely natural eyes of sight and our minds. Jesus himself said that only His disciples could comprehend His teachings on the Kingdom, most of which were presented in cryptic symbolic language, such as in parables. Outsiders would be naturally blinded to these truths, by the direct will of God. The truths of the Kingdom must be spiritually discerned by revelation and enlightened understanding of the Scriptures in our spirit, and learned through experiences of obedience in faith. The Kingdom is very difficult to teach to someone. Rather, it must be experientially lived!

The Kingdom is established within our triune beings—body, mind, and spirit—through surrender and obedience to Jesus as the Son of God Almighty. The Kingdom *is* Jesus ruling as King in the obedient lives of His sons and daughters collectively, and is not a religious system of do's and don'ts. The Kingdom applies in a *general* sense to the affairs of the entire universe. But in a *particular* sense, it is only fully manifested or realized through individuals who voluntarily submit to Jesus as their King. Thus, there is a general involuntary component where the Kingdom governs over all of history, and there is a *voluntary* component in which the sons and daughters are yielded to the King of kings as His subjects. It is to the latter point that we should focus our attention.

Let me further explain why the Kingdom of God is not about Christianity, the religion. God does not desire for us to dwell in the realm of *religion*. Rather, a *relationship* with childlike faith is what God desires from us. *"It is for freedom that Christ has set us free"* (Gal. 5:1a). We are not to be slaves to religion or a religious system, even if it is affiliated with Jesus' teachings. The freedom we enjoy in Jesus comes from being in a relationship in which we are forgiven for our sins and we walk together into righteousness and holiness. Religion always seeks to produce enslavement to a system of rules and rulers. Religion can never produce freedom.

The amusing rhyming lines of Dr. Seuss' "I Had Trouble in Getting to Sola Sollew" reveals the thoughts of someone subjected to unwarranted external control:

> *(he said)…"This is called teamwork. I furnish the brains.*
> *You furnish the muscles, the aches, and the pains."*
> *Then he sat and he worked with his brain and his tongue*
> *and he bossed me around just because I was young.*
> *He told me go left. He told me go right.*
> *And that's what he told me all day and all night.*

Similar to the lines of this enlightening poem, religion produces enslaved subjects who are bossed around by that particular system's leaders, such as pastors, priests, rabbis, mullahs, or professors. Religions produce systematic theologies with traditions and commandments, resulting in legalism and eventually the enslavement of the individual's own captive thoughts. If propagated over time, even the descendants of the religiously infected easily succumb to the same religious errors and traditions. Religious systems tell us to go left; tell us to go right; and that's what they tells us all day and all night!

Religions never produce peace or freedom. It doesn't matter which type of religion one chooses, they *all* fail to produce peace or freedom. Those truths are found only in relationship to Jesus. Religion may provide some helpful guidelines and boundaries for behavior in society, but it can never tear down spiritual strongholds. Religion can provide some restraint in society, as it is better than the alternative, anarchy. But it cannot effectively wage *good* spiritual warfare. As a matter of fact, religion is often engaged in spiritual warfare, albeit on the *wrong* side of the battle!

The following story can help illuminate this crisis of *religion* within the church. A small girl holds the hand of her grandmother as they walk into a well-established bakery in the market district of their town. The nostalgic market district has historic cobblestone pavement, red brick facades, and various cute shops carrying most of the merchandise necessary to maintain life for the town's citizenry. As they stand at the counter in the bakery, the little girl tugs at her grandmother's hand, and asks, "Why does that sign say that the bread is five days old?" The grandmother answers the child with a dismissive remark. So, the girl asks again, "Grandmother, why is all of the bread five days old?" The grandmother replies, "Oh, be at rest my dear; you don't understand. All the bread is five days old in this shop. And, if we want to purchase any bread in town, this is all that is offered to us." The small girl ponders this odd answer for a moment and then replies, "But won't it be stale, hard, and lack flavor?" The grandmother says, "It is either this bread or none at all! We do need to eat something, don't we?" The wise little girl replies for the last time, "Grandmother, many years ago when you were a small girl like me, wasn't the bread baked and served fresh each day?"

The moral of this story is – religion is not fresh bread. Rather, it is like old bread intentionally made using a preservative. It is far easier for most people to live off of predictable five-day-old stale bread (religious traditions) than the present rhema Word of God in true relationship with Jesus, which is like fresh manna. My friends, don't you want His fresh manna today? Don't you want to hear His current *now* voice?

Most local churches in the world today are operating in religious and traditional systems that are vastly removed from their intended purposes to focus on the Kingdom of God. They are essentially local "religious kingdoms," separate from the King, even though lip service is paid to the King as "Lord." It is amusing to contemplate a dialog between an itinerant preacher and God during the preacher's first visit to a congregation. Before speaking, the visiting preacher receives four instructions from the senior pastor and elders, including: (1) that he needs to be careful not to talk about certain Scriptures, as that would likely offend a wealthy lady in the front row of the church, who coincidentally is likely to donate to their building campaign; (2) that he needs to encourage the congregation to dress "more appropriately" in order to be "reverent" before God; (3) that he needs to keep his remarks to the customary limit of 17 minutes or else two of the elders might object if anyone were to nod off; and (4) that he shouldn't raise his hands in a manner that would be considered as "inappropriate for an orderly service." This guest preacher is quite bothered by these restrictive comments. So he goes before God in prayer, "Oh God, why is Your Holy Spirit being stifled in this place?" To which God replies, "My son, I don't know. I have never been invited there."

The Kingdom of God operates when Jesus' will operates through the resident Holy Spirit within His disciples. It isn't about credentials, where you were educated, or whom you know. We don't have to come to Him with seminary degrees or signed "letters" of commendation from a former local church; we just need to come to Him like trusting children expecting our Father to take care of our needs. Having experienced college for more than eight years while earning a Ph.D., and serving as a professor and scientist, I appreciate the value of higher education. A formal education in biblical studies or related theological topics can be quite helpful to many people desiring to serve in ministries. However, I also recognize that having intelligence or a higher degree does not prepare a way for anyone to approach the Almighty God, who knows everything. We are not infinite, yet He is. We know very little, yet He knows everything. God cannot be placed in a box, yet many of our Western churches' seminary-trained pastors and theologians have wrapped Him into a tidy little package of their own denominational understanding. God cannot be contained by the thoughts and doctrines of man, be they ever so grand and polished! We need to return to the Bible as the sole standard and arbiter, not the doctrines of denominations, which have served the devil's strategies well for millennia.

The Kingdom of God does not consist of the religious traditions of denominations. Rather, the Kingdom consists of faith-led devoted disciples following Jesus in trust and obedience. Denominations shall pass away. And, many doctrines shall pass away. But, the Word of God shall last for eternity.

The Church in the world today is long overdue for a major wake-up call! The Church as many of us know it, is in desperate need of repentance, restoration, and returning to biblical truth. My friend Howard Morgan provocatively teaches that "Christianity," as is commonly practiced by many people, is an *aberrant religion*. Much of what is done "in the name of the Lord" has no resemblance to the truths of the Bible. The Church in general is not in a healthy state at present.

One great leader who expressed tremendous courage speaking against the errors of Christian denominationalism was China's Watchman Nee. He detested denominational divisions within Christianity and wrote to his local denomination's leadership:

> "We have seen that sects are unscriptural and that denominationalism is sinful (see 1 Corinthians 1:10-13). Therefore, please remove our names from your book of life. We are doing this not because of any personal animosity, but simply because we wish to obey the Scriptures." (*Watchman Nee – Man of Suffering* by Bob Laurent, Barbour Publishing Inc. Uhrichsville, Ohio, 1998, p. 44)

In addition, concerning the distinction of Christian religion without the substance of real relationship with God, this man familiar with tremendous suffering said:

> "Show the world the fruits of Christianity, and it will applaud; show it Christianity and it will oppose it vigorously. For let the world evolve as it will it can never produce one Christian. A so-called Christian civilization like yours...[referring to the Western World]...gains the recognition and respect of the world. The world can tolerate that; it can even assimilate and utilize that. But Christian life—the life of Christ in the believer—that it hates; and wherever the world meets it, it will oppose it to the death." (*Watchman Nee – Man of Suffering* by Bob Laurent, Barbour Publishing Inc., 1998, p. 96)

I would love to have known this courageous man of God, who was strategically positioned in one of the most difficult countries in the early 20th century! I believe that I share some of Watchman's passions for genuine devotion to Jesus Christ, as opposed to mere religious practices *per se*.

Ironically, being a Christian or for that matter a pseudo-Christian within a Western church in many ways actually works against building up our faith. Many churches have a system that replaces the need for risk-taking belief in action with the security, social gratification, head knowledge, spoon-fed information, structured policies, reinforcement, comfort, regularity, and predictability of an *organization*. The schematic of a typical Western church often resembles a corporation with departments of activities and functions, whose intended purpose can actually unintentionally negate the need for faith. Do you see the irony? The church is supposed to encourage us to walk toward risk-taking belief in action, not provide a safety net to insure that we won't need to face risks. Genuine faith does not come about by default or by following the structure or programs of an organization. We must voluntarily agree to seek it out and abrogate the fear we experience. One revealing sidebar comment about the structure of the Western church was shared by a friend, Doru Cirdei, a key leader in Moldova in Eastern Europe: "Christianity started as a fellowship of believers in Jerusalem; then became a philosophy in Greece; then became a religion in Rome; and finally became a business in America!" This is so sad; the genuine Church is not a business or organization or building. The genuine Church is the Body of Christ revealed within His redeemed sons and daughters.

THE 80:20 PRINCIPLE

Based on experience traveling and speaking around the USA and other nations, I have found one of the greatest deceptions pertains to who are the genuine Christian believers. When people and surveys claim that a high percentage of Americans are "Christians," I have serious reservations that those numbers are anywhere close to the truth. I speculate that the 80:20 principle might be in operation. If this is true, for every 100 people who claim to be "Christians," perhaps 20 have repented and accepted salvation in Jesus as genuine *believers*. The remaining majority might have had some church experience or religious tradition, even if it is frequent, yet they don't really know the Savior. They often can't explain even the simplest of biblical truths, such as the concept of salvation by grace. Most of these 80 individuals think the individuals' spirits will make it to Heaven based on their own good deeds.

Then, of the 20 genuine believers, perhaps only 20 percent of them are genuine *disciples* of Jesus...or thus, only four individuals are surrendered to His will on a routine basis in their lives. And finally, of those four disciples, only approximately one of them is a genuine *spiritual leader!* If the 80:20 principle is true at all three levels, then of 100 people in America today claiming to be "Christians," only one is likely to be a risk-taking faith leader in the Kingdom of God. If this is true, the church in America has a long way to go, in spite of a perception domestically and abroad that we are a "Christian" nation. Believers in America should be drawn to repentance on behalf of the nation. *[Coincidentally, if I recall correctly it has been reported that Bob Jones (the prophet from North Carolina) once encountered an after-death experience in which his spirit ascended to Heaven. In this prophetic experience, He observed that only a few percent of the people on Earth who had died at that time were granted entry into Heaven.]*

Jesus said that you would know His followers (disciples) by their *fruit* and *love* (see Mt. 7:16; Jn. 15:2). If there is no fruit, then you must question the foundational principles of an individual's life, regardless of the words that come out of their mouths or the results of a survey. The "church" is full of pretenders and posers. The wheat and the tares are interspersed. The fruit and love are very difficult to counterfeit, whereas spiritual gifts and spoken words can be more easily counterfeited to look and sound fine. We should discern and judge based more upon the evidences of fruit and the love, and less on the spiritual giftings and an individual's comments.

Much of this problem rests with the leadership of local churches. Although some seminaries are honorable and are concerned with training godly men and women, many seminaries in this time are seriously flawed. These errant seminaries produce spiritually dead leaders. They are infected with disbelief and a lot of head knowledge, without instilling the fear of the Lord. Those defective "infected" seminary products in turn infect their listeners in local congregations within their sphere of influence with lethal deceptions, half-truths, and overt lies that destroy the potential for genuine faith and relationship with God. Those toxic seminaries (or perhaps they should be termed as "cemeteries") and the products thereof should be avoided at all cost. Make no mistake about it, those errant leaders are at the front lines commanding the enemies of the Kingdom of God. Some of them are popular leaders held in high esteem by many. Men and women with regal gowns and dog collars stand proudly in front of the congregation. They are backed up by prestigious seminary degrees in theology, with the evidence prominently hanging on the office wall. Current and potential leaders should be tested by discerning disciples. Many of these leaders are not what they seem to be on the surface. In the poem "The Flaming Heart" by Richard Crashaw, are a few lines concerning being misled by someone:

> ...Readers, be rul'd by me; and make
> Here a well-plac't and wise mistake.
> You must transpose the picture quite,
> And spell it wrong to read it right...

If a leader in the church does not know, obey, and teach the truth of the Bible, then we must be discerning and cautious concerning our willingness to be led by them. They can be dangerous leaders in spite of the way they look or the words they speak, no matter how compassionate and comforting. Jesus isn't interested in us merely knowing the truth; He's interested in whether we're obedient to the truth that we know. Jesus sternly warned us, "*Watch out for false prophets. They come to you in sheep's clothing, but inwardly they are ferocious wolves. By their fruit you will recognize them*" (Mt. 7:15-16a, emphasis added; also see Lk. 13:6-9). We are admonished to test the leaders *vis-a-vis* the truths revealed in the Scriptures (see 1 Jn. 4). Look for the fruit!

The problems are not limited to the leadership. There are many "Polly Anna" followers in the church today. They take everything that they are taught at face value without being a good Berean and checking it out for agreement to biblical truth. We must stop being immature and grow up (see Heb. 6:1-2). We must be responsible for our own beliefs during this life. It is inevitable that we will be accountable in the afterlife. All believers shall be held accountable by the Lord Jesus for whomever they voluntarily submit themselves. If to good leadership, then they are to be commended. But, if to flawed leadership, they should seek immediate remedy. We shall be accountable for which "shepherds" we chose to follow within the Church. Not all of them are to be trusted as reliable leaders. Thus, both the leaders and the followers will be accountable for their actions.

THE FALLACIES OF *PASTOR-LAITY DIVISION* AND *FULL-TIME MINISTRY*

A major problem is the principle of the *pastor-laity division* that is reinforced in most Western churches. You know what I mean—a designated ministry leader up front, over everyone else (i.e., the laymen) in a superior vs. subordinate relationship. The Nicolaitans were detestable to God (see Rev. 2:6,15) because they championed this concept of pastor-laity division...of superiority by the leadership over the people. Instead, in the Scriptures, all believers are called to be ministers and "priests," not just the seminary-trained or full-time pastoral staff. We all are called to an inverted pyramid, where the greatest leaders among us serve the least among us, just as Jesus did in the famous foot washing of His disciples (i.e., His students).

If you are a paid pastor, hang on to your hat! You might find what is revealed in this chapter as either positively exhilarating or unsettling, depending on whether you operate from a perspective of *control* over the flock in your care. The Western church has done a great disservice by the arbitrary creation of the pastor-laity split, as if there are people who are supposed to be holy or religious in their professional careers, while all others are supposed to be secular in their careers. This division is artificial, unnecessary, and harmful. The "set apart" Levitical priesthood of the Hebrew Scriptures is no longer in effect, now that the crucified Christ has been established as the Head over everything within the Church. If we were to seek the full counsel of the Lord from His Word and with a Hebraic mind-set, then we would see that everything we do with our hands and minds is intended for the glory of God. We would see that all we do is part of the spiritual fabric of our existence, whether preaching the gospel to hundreds or merely washing our dirty laundry. We should not reinforce a sacred-secular split in our minds. Rather, *all* that we do should focus on advancing the Kingdom of God. We should not view the full-time pastors or ministers as performing *sacred* works, while the rest of us perform *secular* works. Everything that all believers in the Body of Christ do should be considered as part of His Kingdom's activities. Nothing should be exempted from being *sacred* to us, including our jobs and how we allocate our time and resources.

Few people realize that the pastor-laity split is insidious with grave consequences. One result is that it reinforces the element of *control* by pastoral staff, and *manipulation* in extreme cases. The Protestant Reformation, initially led by the courageous Martin Luther, was in large part a revolution against an erroneous pastor-laity hierarchical concept by the Roman Catholic Church. The *us vs. them* system sought to keep all commoners spiritually "barefoot, pregnant, and ignorant." The Roman Church didn't want individuals to read and understand the logos Word of God for themselves. Nor did the Catholic leaders want individuals to know that salvation is a free gift of God, if in fact any of them even knew this truth during those very dark days when Holy Spirit revelation was hard to find.

The Catholic religious system of oppressive power forced the commoners to be reliant on the local priests (and their superiors) for insight, counsel, and a form of "pseudo-salvation" by good works, acts of repentance and penitence, and financial contributions to the Catholic Church. It was intended to keep the people from never questioning their authorities. That concept was wrong then, and it is still wrong today, not only with regard to Roman Catholicism, but all religions for that matter. We should oppose the very idea and set the captives free, who are blinded by this deception. We should empower and equip every man, woman, and child to know the Bible, to get saved by grace alone, and to become a disciple of Jesus, and then to mature into a minister effectively using his or her own unique spiritual giftings. *[Please note that biblical errors are not exclusive to the Roman Catholic heritage. There are plenty of errors in other Christian denominations and other non-Christian religions as well. I jokingly refer to myself as an equal opportunity critic! If a belief or action is counter to the Bible, then we should be prone to expose it.]*

Purpose and glory in the church are not exclusively reserved for the professional career pastor or minister, who receives a salary based on the benevolence of others. The authority, responsibility, and glory of the Kingdom of God shall be dispersed amongst His disciples. I know of some businessmen and businesswomen who have effective ministries, and in some cases more so than some pastors in local churches. What we should desire is to raise up all believers into God-honoring, surrendered disciples, regardless of whether they have an official role or office (e.g., pastor, elder, deacon, etc.) within the local church.

We should stop encouraging this dichotomy, whereby all youth who are "on fire for God" and desire to serve the Lord are automatically encouraged to go to seminary and *full-time ministry*. Then, their desire is to become a full-time paid minister drawing salary support based on the benevolence of others. This is a man-made Western church concept; you'll have an extremely difficult time defending it in the Bible! Rather, permit young believers/disciples to develop along many diverse career paths, and recognize that God will use the secular world to train almost all of them very effectively for their ministry. If the local church is ill equipped for the task of discipling and training potential "ministers," it might be worth considering seminary training for some, and for those individuals the choice of a Bible-based seminary is critical.

Bi-vocational careers should be highly encouraged! There is nothing inherently wrong with bi-vocationalism, whereby we work a job to make an income and do our ministry activities when not on that job. When training young missionaries and pastors in India for instance, I exhort them to have bi-vocational skills. They need to stop relying on Western financial charity support. They need to support themselves and their own ministries, if at all possible. They need to use genuine faith that does not involve presuming that Westerners will financially "float their boat." I'm pleased that Reaching Indians Ministries International has implemented a strategic bi-vocational skills course within their missionary and pastor training programs at the Mission India Bible Institute (MIBI) in Nagpur in Central India. The beautiful, state-of-the-art MIBI campus was designed by a man of faith, my friend and architect Bob Schill, who is a leader of Missionary Tech Team. Mission India desires that all the students who attend primarily for training in biblical skills will secondarily learn practical work skills for the potential of self-employment. These additional practical skills produce two obvious outcomes, humility and the potential for generating needed resources.

I've often observed an unfortunate attitude by pastors in some regions who feel that manual work is "below them," and that their ministry tasks are superior to other laborers who hold secular jobs. This happens commonly in Third World regions. The root problems are pride and ignorance of the whole counsel of the Lord in the Scriptures. We are to be servant leaders, not arrogant and self-important titled ministers. One song hits the nail on the head, "If you want to be great in God's Kingdom, learn to be the servant of all." Remember that Jesus washed feet, fed the hungry, cried with the weary, raised the dead to life, healed the sick, confronted the religious oppressors, and showed compassion on the less fortunate. None of those actions sound like a man who considered himself as better than anyone else. May we be more like Jesus!

A thorough analysis of biblical teachings on financial support for the concept of paid ministers is very revealing. I highly encourage you to do some research on this topic. Paul, the apostle (a minister of the highest rank in the Kingdom of God) and writer of two thirds of the New Testament, himself worked at manual labor so as not to be a *burden* to other believers (see 2 Cor. 11:9; 12:11-16; 1 Thess. 2:6-9; 4:11-12; 2 Thess. 3:6-15). Surely the apostle Paul was entitled to living off of others' contributions, but he had a servant's heart. He did not "lord it over them." Yes, it is good for deserving ministers to be paid for their labors, but our Western church has erred by overemphasizing this point! Where is the spirit of volunteerism and self-support? A new standard of ministry is being raised up in these days consisting of financial responsibility, self-supporting ministries, marketplace anointings, and generosity...all done by men and women with jobs or who own businesses! The Church must wake up to the new realities and for the need to wisely invest financial resources at the feet of true apostolic-prophetic leaders.

Too many people who desire to be honoring to God presume that they must become a *full-time* minister and work *on staff* of a church. In my opinion in the majority of cases, this is an erroneous misunderstanding. Believers need to know that God can and will use them effectively even in so-called secular careers. We don't need more believers in local churches heading off to seminaries! Rather, we need more believers trained with the help of local churches and ministries, in order to become authentic disciples within their current circumstances. They don't need to leave their current locations, careers, and family relationships in order to be effective in the Kingdom of God. Most just need to *get a job!* I am appalled at the number of well-intentioned young adults who are begging for financial support from other Christians. Some of them are even backed by well-known Christian non-profit organizations, which are encouraging these youth to "live by faith." However, in practice it more closely resembles *presumption* that their family and friends should support them financially, whether they are spiritually mature and deserving of support or not. Please stop it! Most young believers simply need a job, and preferably one that is full-time, and hopefully with the potential to develop their skills. Most of these potential *seminary candidates* need to work with their hands and minds and grow in the disciplines of life.

We also hear some young believers say a remark resembling this, "I need to 'find myself' and the will of God for my life. I'm going to withdraw from society and live in the woods for one year until I find myself." Folks, I consider this to be utter nonsense. Oh! Where is the wisdom of this day? They need a job, so that they can grow in responsibility and service their debts, if any. You can *find yourself* while flipping hamburgers, or mowing grass, painting a house, or writing computer code as an employee...all of which can generate cash. The Scriptures are full of examples encouraging diligent hard work to ward off laziness (e.g., Prov. 12:11,24,27; Prov. 21:5,25-26; 2 Thess. 3:6-15). I sure hope that the young readers of this book will take special note of this warning! In the parable of the talents, we learn that God will not entrust His valuable possessions to those who have not lived responsibly and have not passed their lesser tests (see Mt. 25). Withdrawing into the woods or a monastic experience is not God's general will for us. Sure, short-term spiritual retreats away from the busy-ness of life have considerable value for us. But, we must be *"in the world but not of it"* in order to have an impact as salt and light in a dark world for the Kingdom of God. Please listen—the "church" has been in gross error on these two issues of *pastor-laity split* and *full-time ministry* for quite a long time. It is time for an enlightened new generation to move beyond those hindrances of the past.

If a "secular" job was good enough for the apostle Paul, then a job is good enough for *all* other believers. No one is exempt by Paul's biblical life example of working a job to be self-supporting and so as to not be burdensome to others. That is a shocking revelation to many. I can personally testify that my "secular" career track has opened doors of opportunity in ministry and influence around the world that would seldom be opened to a typical full-time salaried pastor. The numerous adverse circumstances and successes of a job produce character within us. They make us highly relevant to other people in our peer group. Please listen! Something is dramatically wrong with the Western church in this regard. We all need to be ministers, not just the "ministers" *per se!* Furthermore, we need to develop a Hebraic mind-set in which we consider everything that we do is done unto the Lord. The artificial distinction between *sacred* and *secular* must be abandoned, and everything that we do must be done in a righteous and holy manner.

SECRETS OF THE *INVISIBLE* KINGDOM OF GOD

The Kingdom of God and "Christianity," as most of us know it, are not the same thing. What we see on the surface of the religion of "Christianity" often has very little to do with biblical teachings on the Kingdom of God. Have you considered how many teachings on the Kingdom of God spoken by Jesus are described in *invisible* or *concealed* symbolic terms?

- How about seeds planted and hidden in the soil...so tiny, yet capable of yielding a giant plant or tree bearing fruit after its kind (see Mk. 4:26-34)?

- How about the buried treasure in a field worth selling everything one owns to possess it (see Mt. 13:44)?

- How about a beautiful pearl of great price concealed within an ugly oyster shell (see Mt. 13:45-46)?

- How about living yeast cells that are too small to be seen by the naked eye? Doesn't it need a microscope to be visible, yet one tiny yeast cell can eventually ferment a large batch of bread dough (see Mt. 13:33)?

- How about the small silver coin that the woman knew was lost somewhere in her home, but she couldn't see it, and it caused great anxiety until it was recovered (see Lk. 15:8-10)?

- How about the father whose eyes searched the horizon for the return of his lost prodigal son, while he was still a long way from home, and while the father still had a dutiful son remaining at home (see Lk. 15:11-31)?

- How about the shepherd who searched for one lost sheep, while he had 99 other sheep in safety at home (see Lk. 15:1-7)?

By these examples isn't Jesus instructing us that the Kingdom of God consists at least in part of things that *must* be appropriated by faith in the *unseen realm*? With few exceptions, the Kingdom of God does not consist of *visible* religious traditions and rituals, which we can see and touch and perform. We must take action on that which is unseen and believe it to be true. The farmer invested the seeds into the soil expecting a harvest in the future; the treasure hunters sold everything to possess the buried treasure or the pearl of great value; the woman searched diligently until she located the lost coin; the shepherd searched for the lost animal; and the prodigal's father sought him out. Do you see this truth now? Great importance is placed on "seeing" that which is unseen, concealed, or lost. We must then walk toward it. That is faith, whereas pursuit of religion is not. Religion largely operates within the *seen* realm, whereas faith always operates in the *unseen* realm! The Kingdom of God is exercised within us by our obedience to walk in faith.

APOSTOLIC-PROPHETIC RESTORATION

God established the principle of the five-fold ministry in the Book of Ephesians to facilitate the building up of the Church for establishment of the Kingdom:

> *It was He who gave some to be **apostles**, some to be **prophets**, some to be **evangelists**, and some to be **pastors** and **teachers**, to prepare God's people for works of service, so that the body of Christ may be built up until we all reach unity in the faith and in the knowledge of the Son of God and become mature, attaining to the whole measure of the fullness of Christ* (Ephesians 4:11-13, emphasis added).

Genuine apostles and prophets trained with the giftings of "spiritual" discernment and prophetic insights can guide in the process of separating the truth from the lie. Discerning and wise apostles and prophets have enhanced abilities to listen to rhema revelation, and have different spiritual giftings than most pastors. Thus, apostolic-prophetic leaders form part of the foundational layer of the Kingdom adjacent to the Cornerstone, Jesus (see Eph. 2:20). All other callings and positions of the Church are built upon their forerunner ministries. The apostles and prophets help lead local evangelists, pastors, and teachers. Apostles and prophets police error, deception, and presumption within the local church and worldwide. True apostolic-prophetic leaders also provide direction and guidance toward the future of the Church. They provide strategies for spiritual warfare to advance the Kingdom. Not only was the Church built historically upon the labors and words of the ancient apostles and prophets, but is still to this day *being* built upon the labors and words of the apostles and prophets. It will continue to be built upon their labors and words until the Church age is completed.

We need restoration of the genuine apostolic-prophetic order within local churches! *Pastoral* giftings, though necessary and very good at the local church level, are not sufficient. Most churches today are controlled by a single individual leader with a pastoral or teaching gift, who is often reluctant to recognize and come into alignment with God's intended five-fold ministry purposes. Our institutional and denominational policies further reinforce Christian "religion," which is typically controlled at the pastoral level, as opposed to the Kingdom of God. Pastors need apostles and prophets to speak into their lives and to bring accountability. When the genuine apostolic-prophetic order arrives in force on Earth, the Kingdom of God will rapidly grow in Holy Spirit power. Then, local pastors will be blessed by the support and complementary giftings of other leaders.

I have often heard many of the leading voices of the church growth movement declare the following statement, "The local church is the hope for the world!" Most of the advocates for this phrase are pastors of local churches with good intentions to spread the gospel of Jesus and to promote growth through addition of new local communities of believers. I believe that although there is some truth in this statement, it is misleading. A more correct statement is, "The Kingdom of God is the hope for the world." The reason that the former statement is misleading is that it reinforces the perception that *all* that God is doing is being done at the *local church* level, which is typically overseen by local pastors. Sure, the local church is a major component of the Kingdom. But, the former statement reinforces pastoral control often to the exclusion of apostolic-prophetic order at a higher level and of ministries reaching beyond the local congregation level. The Kingdom of God is a vastly bigger umbrella than the local churches collectively. There are many holes or gaps not being filled directly by local congregations that can only be effectively addressed at the higher level.

Please give careful attention to these radical thoughts. Be a good "Berean" (see Acts 17:11), and check them out for yourself in the Bible and via the indwelling Holy Spirit. We need to enter this season of the latter end with the authority of the Church resting upon the shoulders of genuine Holy Spirit-led apostles and prophets with power, not just on the shoulders of pastors of local congregations, as many have been doing for centuries. I appreciate the relatively recent emphasis on the need for restoration of apostolic-prophetic order by leaders such as Howard Morgan, Chuck Pierce, Bill Hamon, and Jim Goll. Read or listen to some of their teachings for further illumination on this critical topic for our days.

We need to exhort all genuine believers to cast their resources (time, talents, and treasures) at the feet of genuine apostolic-prophetic leaders (see Acts 4:32–5:2), who are best suited to discern the "big picture" of needs of the entire Kingdom of God worldwide, as opposed to merely the local needs of a single local congregation. At present, the vast majority of funding in the church is controlled and distributed by local pastors. The bigger picture overseen by genuine apostles is not sufficiently established and funded. Very little money is currently in the hands of apostolic-prophetic leaders who demonstrate the supernatural power of God routinely. Unfortunately, we have the cart before the horse!

This sad state of affairs is further complicated by local facilities' *building campaigns* that unnecessarily tie up millions of dollars of resources in building huge ornate "cathedrals," that could otherwise meet more worthy and pressing needs of people within and outside of the local congregation. Recently I experienced a disturbing spiritual dream in which many paupers in simple woolen garments were huddled together for collective warmth on the back two rows of a huge ancient European cathedral. A spokesman for them arose and cried out loud in despair for assistance as they shivered in extreme cold. Yet, no one helped them! There were many "demonic" bats flying around the high ceiling of this giant beautiful masonry cathedral, as if to mock the paupers' pathetic hopeless situation that mirrored the Dark Ages of Europe. The cathedral was a place of cold and death, my friends! The cathedral was not a place of salt and light to a perishing world. There was no warmth, no love, and no rescuing those in great need.

[Note there is an inherent warning in this dream for the modern Church, and especially in Europe. I have been increasingly burdened by routine spiritual dreams about the immoral darkness and rejection of Judeo-Christian truth that is rapidly destroying Europe. As an observer of the Kingdom of God in various nations, I say to you my friends - the United Kingdom is very close behind Europe, and the USA is not far behind the UK. I have already seen very dark days ahead for Europe. Believers, rise up now!]

Nowhere in the New Testament does it command or advise local churches to *build* temples or church facilities. Yet, to most Western Christians' way of thinking it seems that it is a foregone conclusion and an absolute necessity. In the Scriptures, the first-century believers met wherever convenient, in homes, outdoors, or in local Jewish synagogues that permitted them to do so. I'm not saying that facilities are not useful and helpful in many cases, but the perceived *need* for local church buildings (and especially extravagant facilities) must be balanced with regard to *all other needs* of the local congregation and global Church. The explicit pattern of the New Testament was to focus first upon the needs of the believers. It is worth noting that rapid growth of the Church worldwide has often happened during times of intense persecution. Often that meant that access to permanent facilities were denied or suppressed, such as in China over the past century. Local congregations can grow in spite of not having a permanent facility. Please question your own priorities. Church buildings are *optional*, but other needs are not. Too often leaders of local churches have not discerned the difference between a *want* and a *need*. Too often they have just assumed that the facilities are the focal point driving the ministry. A ministry built in the flesh, must be maintained in the flesh. A ministry built in the Spirit, must be maintained in the Spirit. I would rather have the latter.

Therefore, we should meet others' *needs* before our own *wants!* There are numerous biblical mandates that are un-funded because of local building programs, such as food for the poor, world missions, effective so-called "para-church" ministries, etc. We are really missing this one big time. Shame on us! Please, I urge you, reconsider how your time, talents, and treasures are allocated within the context of the greater Kingdom of God. Are you giving generously to your local church? And, are you giving financially to the true apostolic-prophetic leaders of the Church?

APOSTOLIC-PROPHETIC LEADERS ARE ESSENTIAL, BUT THEY ARE NOT PERFECT

When a genuine prophet or apostle grows in prophetic gifting through many steps of faith and testing, it becomes increasingly clear how to discern His voice. Prophets and apostles are not perfect, and they know only in part and prophesy in part. Individual prophets and apostles aren't always right on everything. At times they say and do the wrong things, because they are human beings and not "gods." Many examples of errant words or actions by prophets or apostles are noted in Scripture; here are six examples to consider:

- The prophet Samuel declared that he would not return with King Saul to worship, after the king sinned overtly and was rejected by God. But, after Saul pleaded in a manipulative manner, Samuel disobeyed his own words and accompanied the king (see 1 Sam. 15).

- Again, the prophet Samuel declared in error, without first hearing from the Lord, that Eliab was *"surely the Lord's anointed,"* when God intended for the youngest son of Jesse, David, to be anointed (see 1 Sam. 16).

- The prophet Jonah initially refused to yield to God's prompting to bring the word of repentance to the Assyrians in the city of Ninevah. He later repented after encountering severe discipline (see Jonah 1–4).

- After the superb victory over 850 false prophets of Baal and Asherah at Mount Carmel, the prophet Elijah was threatened by King Ahab and Jezebel. She was the demonic manipulator behind the throne. *"Elijah was afraid and ran for his life."* Out of fear of Jezebel, he pleaded that God would take his life. God questioned and rebuked him. Then Elijah said that he was the only prophet left in the land, which he knew was not true. Elijah knew Obadiah had hidden 100 prophets in two caves (see 1 Kings 18–19). (I've heard Jim Goll speculate that these 100 individuals were serving as hidden prophetic intercessors, while Elijah was at risk on the front lines as a path-clearing prophet.)

- A nameless old prophet intentionally misled another younger prophet as a test to the younger man. The younger prophet disobeyed the word of the Lord given to him as a result of this deceptive test, and disobedience cost him his life (see 1 Kings 13). Please note that is not to say that lying and deception are condoned. But, this example is recorded as a warning to hold fast in obedience to the word that God gives prophetically. It might also indicate that an individual with the gift of prophecy can effectively use the gift even outside of God's will. Spiritual gifts can be in operation within an individual who lacks character.

- The apostle Peter was overtly rebuked by the apostle Paul for error(s) concerning his outward demonstrations of religious conduct, as Peter attempted to please Jewish believers within the early Church. "*When Peter came to Antioch, I [Paul] opposed him to his face, because he was clearly in the wrong*" (Gal. 2:11). Peter had moved from focusing on the relationship with Christ, back to a form of religious Judaism. *[There is a needed current similar warning for some "Messianic Jewish" believers today, who are not only cherishing the Hebraic roots to the Judeo-Christian faith, but some of them are going too far and are practicing syncretism. They are essentially turning from "relationship" to a "religion of Judaism."]*

So, prophets and apostles were (and are) human beings! They are not perfect in all they say or do. In view of the potential for errors in words and deeds, apostolic-prophetic leaders should be accountable to other genuine prophets and apostles. For instance modern prophets should relate to one another within the context of a *school of prophets*, a biblical concept clearly demonstrated during the times of Elijah in the Old Testament and repeated again to one of the local churches in the New Testament (see I Kings 18:13; 1 Cor. 14:29-33). The plurality of similarly-gifted individuals serves to protect the truth of the messages given. Who better to question the inspiration and veracity of a prophetic word spoken by a prophet than another prophet (or prophetic apostle) with a similar spiritual gift? God doesn't want a bunch of "loner" prophets out operating in self-willed independence. His checks-and-balances help to keep the message pure and to protect the "sheep" of His flock from errant words.

CESSATIONISM HINDERS FAITH AND APOSTOLIC-PROPHETIC RESTORATION

Unfortunately, there are many individuals who agree with *cessationist* doctrine (i.e., denial that the Holy Spirit still routinely works today through miraculous spiritual gifts, as in the Book of Acts). Cessationists discount or discard the reality of modern prophecy, prophetic individuals, and prophets. Some of these individuals justify their belief in opposition to the miraculous power of the Holy Spirit in part by holding onto a standard that a prophet must demonstrate absolute perfection concerning their prophetic declarations or actions. This is not the case. There is not a single spiritual gift or calling that demands perfection all the time in its use. Satan has very effectively used cessationist exaggerations and errors about supernatural spiritual gifts (e.g., perfection is required in prophetic ministry and apostolic-prophetic leaders ceased after the first century once the Bible was complete) to blind the eyes of millions of Christians around the world in various denominations.

Fortunately, by direct revelation of the Holy Spirit, many blind eyes are now being opened for the first time to this truth. It takes God's revelation to overcome this error of understanding. Head knowledge of the Bible alone is not effective at abrogating this error. Please note my own somewhat painful journey through this path. I was an active Bible-believing evangelical with at least sympathy toward cessationism for many years. I had been taught this doctrine as a new believer and had accepted it as inspired truth. I had never carefully studied the miraculous giftings in the Scriptures for its veracity as applying in today's world. The arguments against the supernatural manifestations of the Holy Spirit today espoused by my fundamentalist evangelical teachers with cessationist bias just seemed to make sense. However, God Almighty ambushed me with the power of the Holy Spirit, when I wasn't actively seeking it! Many of my readers will also note a similar transition in their own lives. I had formerly viewed the Holy Spirit as a mere *concept*, rather than as a *person* manifesting the miracle-working attributes and faith of God within us.

Concerning the work of the Holy Spirit, I recommend the writings of Dr. Jack Deere and Dr. R.T. Kendall. Dr. Deere was a theologian teaching within a respected evangelical seminary. He experienced a similar progression from a deep appreciation of the logos written Word alone to subsequently an added appreciation for the gifts and power of the Holy Spirit. For instance, please consider his book entitled *Surprised by the Power of the Spirit*. Another fine example to study is the life and writings of Dr. R.T. Kendall, the former Pastor of Westminster Chapel in London, who progressively introduced the works of the Spirit in that congregation. One of his books worth examining is entitled *The Anointing: Yesterday, Today, and Tomorrow*. Both authors provide balanced understandings of the need for both the Word and the power of the Holy Spirit. Both of them experience the benefits of the logos and the rhema. We need more balanced leaders like them in the Church today!

To an unbiased first-time reader of the Bible, it would be obvious that God is a miracle worker throughout from Genesis to Revelation. The presumption would be that this pattern of common miraculous works continues on to this present day. There is no explicit statement in Scripture upon which the cessationist argument can be successfully defended, and in spite of a mountain of evidence to the contrary throughout the Bible. Cessationism is primarily built upon *"negative experiences"* with regard to the miraculous realm. The lack of observation is never a solid justification for a definitive doctrine of denial. Just because someone hasn't personally seen God move miraculously doesn't mean that God does not do so routinely today (e.g., on behalf of other individuals)! Furthermore, Psalm 18:25-27 indicates that our own pre-conceived ideas of how God works will limit our understanding of Him and his potential to act on our behalf. If you don't expect Him to perform miracles routinely, then it is very likely that you shall receive what you are expecting. Those who have genuine faith that God does and will move in the miraculous do see Him move in this fashion far more often than those lacking faith in a miracle-working God.

I agree with Jack Deere that most cessationist beliefs are established by the biased doctrine of theologians and ministers based on the absence of positive experiences with the miraculous, rather than on a careful analysis of the whole counsel of the Scriptures. Just because I can't see with my eyes many forms of electromagnetic radiation (e.g. radio waves, X-rays, etc.), doesn't mean they don't exist. My denial based on personal "negative" observations doesn't negate their presence. You can have religion without Jesus. And you can have Jesus without power. Let us all have both Jesus and power! Consider this from another perspective. You can have religion without the logos Word. And you can have the logos Word without the rhema Word. But, let us all have both. Let us have the Word and the Spirit!

Another argument by the defenders of cessationist theology is that co-called modern prophets are all just "false prophets" or magicians working for the devil. Well, that presents a very interesting dilemma for the proponents. Sure, I don't deny that there are hordes of false prophets in the world today. There are plenty of them, and the numbers are increasing. I encounter and confront them. However, this argument suggests that only satan has enough power to reveal information from the spirit realm, but that God, who has even greater authority and omnipotence, is unwilling to reveal information from the spirit realm to us. That sure seems ironic. That argument merely puts God in a box of our own limited understanding about His nature and actions. My personal experiences (e.g., see Chapter 7) and the Scriptures do not bear witness to that assertion. The Holy Spirit is alive and well and speaking and performing miracles each day! Now is not the time to bury our heads in the sands of denial. We are facing increased spiritual warfare and demonic manifestations in the world. We need God-honoring prophetic disciples to fight in those battles.

We all must grow in our spiritual gifts, and that can involve making mistakes. But, prophetic leaders should have a reliable track record and have demonstrated an apostolic and/or prophetic anointing over many years. There should be evidence of God working through their prophetic words, answering their specific prayers, and blessing them with spiritual fruit of their lives (see Gal. 5). You shall know them by their fruit.

Apostolic-prophetic leaders help guide the Church toward the excellence of discernment needed to lead a community of believers. Discernment and wisdom are necessary to know which Scriptures take priority within a given situation, when it appears that different Scriptures are in conflict with one another. At present it is unfortunate that many Christians do not have reliable discernment of His voice in rhema revelation. Sad to say, many people often are relying on the wrong spiritual gifts and/or callings. For instance, some say, "I am a pastor or teacher or evangelist," or "I know the Bible cover to cover," or "I speak in tongues." Well, it might be a surprise that those spiritual gifts or callings aren't the same as the other gifts of prophecy, discernment, words of knowledge, words of wisdom, and the apostolic calling! Many folks in the church are easily deceived about a lot of things, and reliance on the wrong kind of spiritual gift(s) is an error. Each gifting and calling has its unique purposes.

Prophecy is listed in the New Testament as a supernatural spiritual gift, whereas the roles of apostle or prophet are not spiritual "gifts" *per se*, although these individuals utilize one or more supernatural spiritual gifts within those callings (e.g., prophecy, faith, healing, deliverance, tongues, interpretation of tongues, etc.) along with other more "natural" giftings (e.g., teaching, evangelism, encouragement, compassion, etc.). For instance many people can have a prophetic gift, but far fewer will operate in the calling of the *prophet*. The manifestations of the gift of prophecy are various, but there are two major forms of revelatory expression—*verbal* (e.g., words of knowledge and words of wisdom) and *graphic* (e.g., trances, visions, pictures, and dreams). Therefore, prophetic individuals tend to be stronger in one of the two forms. It is my observation that few disciples in the Church are anointed as *prophets*, and even fewer as *apostles*, regardless of whether anyone grants them the "title" for their calling. Many believers seem to be leery of assigning those two ministry titles, perhaps with good reason in certain cases. I find it ironic that most believers are quick to assign the titles of "evangelist, pastor, or teacher" without hesitation, but they are very tentative concerning the titles of "apostle or prophet," and perhaps for good reason in many cases. However, nowhere in our Scriptures does it explicitly indicate that two of the five ministry callings of Ephesians 4 ceased after the first century.

Therefore, most believers have a more limited prophetic understanding. But, we are admonished by the apostle Paul to desire the supernatural spiritual gifts, and especially the "higher" gift of prophecy (see 1 Cor. 14:1, 39). That is why the Church needs genuine apostolic-prophetic leaders to advance in spiritual warfare to claim new territories for the Kingdom. Both apostles and prophets have a prophetic gift and are experienced in revelatory knowledge. The foundation of the Church is Jesus Christ as the chief cornerstone. And, next to Him on the foundation level are the apostles and prophets (see Eph. 2:20-22). The church is built on Jesus *plus* the apostolic-prophetic leadership.

WHO ARE THE GENUINE APOSTLES?

It is surprising to some Christians that most pastors don't have the callings and giftings of the apostle or prophet. Typically local church ministers (including the senior pastors) have the primary calling of an evangelist, a pastor, or a teacher within the five-fold ministry callings of Ephesians 4. Very seldom are local church pastors also apostles or prophets, in spite of self-serving declarations to the contrary by some of them or by their denominational leadership that they are in the office of "bishop, prophet, overseer, or apostle." Be careful about assigned leadership titles, for they can be misleading and misrepresent the anointing (or lack thereof) for ministry. Conversely, it is also important to note that not all apostles are pastors! A pastoral calling is not a *de facto* growth tract to becoming an apostle. So, churches founded by evangelists, pastors, and teachers without apostolic-prophetic oversight can be houses built on a sandy foundation. The revelatory insights of genuine apostolic-prophetic leaders can serve to help the local church's ministers to discern errors and dangers in the course ahead, and provide a clearer roadmap to fully equip the local church's believers. Apostolic-prophetic leaders are invaluable "resources" for the establishment, growth, and correction of local churches.

So, the $64,000 question then becomes, "Who are the genuine apostles?" It might surprise some readers to note that many (or possibly most) of the apostolic-prophetic leaders operating in Holy Spirit-led authority and power are actually a bunch of nameless, faceless, humble individuals. Some have not been formally recognized in this capacity by the local church. Many of them are not even pastors. Now that's a surprise to many of us! Some of them are businessmen, businesswomen, or entrepreneurs, working primarily outside of so-called full-time ministry. Apostles operate in authority with multiple spiritual gifts, even though they might not be officially recognized for their current "assignments" within the Kingdom of God. Some are on *stealth* assignments by the Holy Spirit's guidance. The sovereign hand of God intentionally holds back some leaders for years while in training. These leaders, intended for apostolic-prophetic ministries, might only be known by their closest spiritual brothers and sisters, and perhaps overlooked by the official church leadership in their region.

Have you ever seriously pondered that Jesus was not formally trained as a Jewish rabbinical priest (at least the Bible doesn't indicate that He was)? He was trained as the son of a carpenter or homebuilder or stonemason. Jesus was a "businessman" and labored with His hands until He was approximately 30 years old! Yet, the whole time He was growing in understanding, wisdom, and power. At the same time He was learning the Law and the Prophets (the books of the Hebrew Bible), and was known in the temple for His wise insights. Furthermore, none of Jesus' chosen initial 12 disciples (apostles) were rabbinical priests. They were laborers of various types. Oh, how quickly we seem to forget the obvious in view of our cultural biases. To the best of our awareness, none of His close friends attended seminary.

The Western "church" has told each of us so much for so long that we haven't stopped to question the biblical relevance of our beliefs. Cessationists propose that only the small number of those who were directly called by Jesus while He walked the Earth 20 centuries ago can qualify as legitimate apostles (e.g., the original 12 plus a few others). Nowhere in Scripture does it say that the calling or position of apostle ceased once the original individuals chosen by Jesus had died. To the contrary there is good evidence in the Scriptures (Acts and Epistles) and extra-biblical sources that the calling continued beyond the replacement of Judas and the miraculous selection of Paul in an "untimely" manner after Jesus' resurrection.

In my opinion, apostles are relatively "rare" leaders among the Church, because it requires a high level of spiritual maturity, multiple spiritual giftings, evidences of supernatural spiritual power, revelatory understanding, and having developed a solid intimate familiarity with Jesus. Even in the Book of Acts, the apostles voted on Judas' replacement, Matthias (see Acts 1:21-26), based upon those disciples who knew Jesus well. So, knowing Him well, either while literally walking on the Earth during the first century or now in the modern era, is a biblical standard for an apostolic calling. Knowing Him well today can be interpreted to be obedient to His voice as His trusted friend. Some of the other disciples mentioned in the New Testament either were or might have been apostles without being termed as such in the text. For instance, some of Paul's other peers were referred to as *apostles*, such as Barnabas and James—the brother of Jesus and apostolic leader in Jerusalem. It is plausible that Andronicus and Junias, Priscilla and Aquila, and Silas (and others) also might have been considered as apostolic-prophetic leaders during the first century.

Note that miracle-working power was very common among the original leaders of the Church, who had been commissioned and anointed with power by Jesus. He sent them out two-by-two to minister, and they experienced first-hand miracles (e.g., healings and deliverance of demonic influences). Why should anyone expect less today from the true apostolic-prophetic leaders of His Church? The Scriptures also provide a snapshot in the future at the end of days, in which two apostolic-prophetic *witnesses* will operate in high-level authority and supernatural power (see Rev. 11:1-6). So, as we rapidly approach the end times, shouldn't we expect the supernatural manifestations of the power of God (see Joel 2:28-32)? The final days of the two "future" witnesses is rapidly arriving. Even if apostles were relatively rare leaders of the Church in history, it does not mean that there are "none" in the world today.

The cessationist philosophy quenches the Holy Spirit and is directly damaging to the development of genuine faith. To argue that the calling of apostle or prophet ceased two millennia ago defies direct evidence of numerous individuals operating with similar giftings and callings today. The cessationist doctrine effectively limits the progression of faith of those who believe in it. It is a self-reinforcing principle. If one believes that miracles do not routinely happen today, then they will not pursue potential miracles in prayer and action. They will receive the results of their "negative faith," if there is such an oxymoronic thing. They shall not observe answered prayers and miracles today on a routine basis. Those who invest "negative faith" shall reap "negative results." You might have heard it said, "If you think you can or you think you cannot, you are correct!" There is a key element of truth in this statement. Without routinely experiencing answered prayers and miracles, most believers are held back by the doctrines and deceptions of the enemy from advancing up the "ladder of faith." In order to advance in Jesus' army in spiritual warfare within the Kingdom, we need believers to grow in faith through experiences of answered prayers and the miraculous. Apostolic-prophetic leaders, by their actions, help stimulate the development of faith within the members of the Church.

God has assigned many apostles and prophets to humbling, lowly, and demeaning positions within local congregations for their training and testing. They are like David hiding in a cave, even though they have received a powerful anointing for service. Ironically, this is in spite of the fact that they have sufficient spiritual authority and giftings that they could perhaps overrule the leadership team of most typical local churches. I believe that God has kept His apostles "under the table" for release at the proper *kairos* time, so that their destinies can be fulfilled. He's kept them in training and in humility for release at a later date. I believe that it is also safe to assume that a fair proportion of the individuals that have already been assigned the official titles of apostle, prophet, or bishop by some local congregation might not in fact be "worthy" of that title or calling. Only God can anoint and equip genuine apostles and prophets.

If you don't know who they are, pray for God to give you discernment to show you who the genuine apostolic-prophetic leaders are with authority in your region and/or your area of ministry. He can point them out to you. You don't need to look in a telephone book or search online for them using those keywords. Some, but not all, pastors are coincidentally apostolic-prophetic leaders and/or they might be accountable to other apostles and prophets who provide oversight. Sure we want excellent pastors, teachers, and evangelists at the local church level, but we also want them to be accountable to genuine apostolic-prophetic leaders.

The *hallmarks of genuine apostles* include:

- Apostles carry an *anointing with power* demonstrated through signs, wonders, miracles, great faith, and prophetic understanding (see Acts 2:43; 5:12). They operate effectively with multiple spiritual gifts. Their tool chest is quite full of diverse natural and supernatural spiritual gifts. If they lack demonstrations of supernatural power (e.g., prophecy, demonic deliverance, or healings), in spite of capabilities in other more natural gifts (e.g., teaching or compassion), you should question whether they are called by God as apostles. Those talented individuals lacking miraculous manifestations can be wonderful leaders in the Church, but are they *really* apostolic leaders? According to Second Corinthians 12:12, evidence of miracle-working power is necessary to qualify as an apostle.

- Apostles have *high-level authority* over geographic regions (e.g., cities, states, provinces, nations) and have effective influence in spiritual warfare. They demonstrate an open door authority with power in those regions of God-assigned influence (see Rev. 3:7-8; Is. 22:22). They courageously serve as path clearers of new territory for other believers to follow in ministry as builders. Their motivation is to maximize impact to the largest extent possible for the Kingdom, but without using unnecessary control and manipulation. They receive rhema revelation about key strategies to build the Kingdom and to wage spiritual warfare.

• Unlike all other spiritual gifts, the apostolic calling *takes many years* in obedient service and training to actually possess it. Many spiritual gifts can be received instantaneously by impartation, and the person can begin to operate in it, even while making a lot of mistakes. If not many of us are to presume to be teachers (see Jas. 3:1) and recent converts shouldn't be pastors (see 1 Tim. 3:6), it certainly follows that apostles will typically take a long time in the fire to be refined for their assigned tasks in that "higher" calling of leadership. It is a leadership "position" requiring abundant faith in obedience to biblical truths over many years. Please meditate on that for a minute!

• A mature apostle exhibits *power masked by humility.* They should have a track record of evidences of Holy Spirit supernatural power, but always backed up by solid character (e.g., integrity and diligence) and love above all else. A minister of the gospel can have supernatural power and still not be a trusted apostle for various reasons. Although genuine apostles have a high rank in the Kingdom of God, they must demonstrate a servant's heart, just as Jesus did on the Earth. Let us be reminded that without love, even the most powerful leader is not seeking God's will (see 1 Cor. 13:1-3).

Jesus said, *"I tell you the truth, unless you change and become like little children, you will never enter the kingdom of heaven. Therefore, whoever humbles himself like this child is the greatest in the kingdom of heaven"* (Mt. 18:3-4). The mark of any disciple, and especially an apostle with regional or global authority, should be to serve others in humility. I recommend Rick Joyner's book *The Final Quest* that portrays a beautiful graphic picture of the mantle of humility cloaking the radiant armor of God on one of His soldiers.

Furthermore, it is not about the assigned official *title* of apostle, general overseer, bishop, etc.; it is about the heart attitude of the individual. Jesus said, *"And do not call anyone on earth 'father,' for you have one Father and He is in heaven. Nor are you to be called 'teacher' for you have one Teacher, the Christ. The greatest among you will be your servant. For whoever exalts himself will be humbled, and whoever humbles himself will be exalted"* (Mt. 23:9-12). Jesus looks at the heart, not the title. We should emulate His example.

OTHER OBSERVATIONS ABOUT THE KINGDOM

One should seriously meditate on the meaning of the *Kingdom of God* (or the *Kingdom of Heaven*). Far too often, it is over-simplified incorrectly to be synonymous with the local church or the Church universal. Although both of these are critical components of the Kingdom, they do not constitute *all* of the Kingdom of God. Doesn't a business owned by a God-honoring disciple belong within the Kingdom? Doesn't a so-called "para-church" organization (e.g., Intervarsity Christian Fellowship or Wycliffe Bible Translators) belong within the Kingdom? Doesn't a group of teenage believers praying before school starts belong within the Kingdom? Doesn't an individual or group with an Isaiah 58 ministry to help the widows, aliens, orphans, and homeless belong within the Kingdom? Doesn't a persecuted lone disciple of Christ in a prison cell in China, India, or the Middle East belong within the Kingdom? Please seek God's logos and rhema confirmation on this issue. The Church must re-discover the true breadth of what the Kingdom is today.

Let us pursue with *agape* love the Kingdom that Jesus taught. Let us flow in the river of the Holy Spirit as He leads us by His faith deeper into the waters of the Kingdom of God. In the future the following truth shall be revealed, *"The kingdom of the world **has become** the kingdom of our Lord and of His Christ, and He will reign for ever and ever"* (Rev. 11:15b, emphasis added). May we hasten the day that the Kingdom of God is established on Earth as in Heaven, with Jesus reigning over everyone and everything! As we *"live by faith of the Son of God"* (see Gal. 2:20), His Kingdom will be advanced on Earth.

Chapter Ten

QUESTIONS

1. What is the Kingdom of God? Is it present tense, future tense, or both?

2. List the major overlaps and differences between the Kingdom of God, the local church, and the Church universal.

3. Does God *always* use local churches for His intended plans to evangelize, disciple, and equip within the world?

4. Do you believe that *false* "apostles and prophets" exist in the Church and world today? If not, then why not? Have you encountered any of them?

5. Do you believe that *true* "apostles and prophets" exist in the Church today? If not, then why not? Have you encountered any of them?

6. Why has there been ignorance and/or resistance to the establishment of apostolic-prophetic authority and leadership in the Church?

7. Are certain "leaders" in the Church threatened or fearful of apostolic-prophetic restoration and authority? If so, whom and why?

8. Why is there no place for "competition and control" within the Kingdom of God?

9. If you are a believer, how have your beliefs about theology been formed and restricted by a Christian denomination?

List both the benefits and disadvantages to the denomination that has most impacted your life.

10. Has this been a provocative chapter? What did you most like and dislike?

11. If believers genuinely listened to and obeyed Jesus' commands, what major changes would Jesus require of your local church or ministry?

12. How many believers are necessary to make up a local church?

Chapter One

ENDNOTES

LIFE OF A CENTURION IN ROMAN JUDEA

During Jesus' life in Judea two millennia ago, most of the Western World was under the dominion of the Roman Emperor, Tiberius. Roman imperial governance was at the top of the authority pyramid, but other recognized authority structures were also in operation in various regions, such as in Judea. By effective military force the emperor's government controlled the trade routes of the Mediterranean including North Africa, Judea, Asia Minor, and a large portion of Europe. One of the most critical trade routes was the Via Maris highway through Judea and connecting to Egypt in the west and to the Euphrates River in the north and east.

In addition to the Roman occupiers in Judea, Herod the Great and his descendants reigned as a quasi-Jewish Kingdom, although not purely of Hebraic lineage. These tyrants' loyalties focused on appeasing Rome for personal benefit in a codependent relationship of authority and oppression of the local Jewish peoples. Jesus was a child in a village overlooking one of Herod's impressive palaces. The Herodians with loyalties to Rome were in conflict with the religious leaders of the Jewish temple in Jerusalem and the peoples of Judea. Thus, Jesus interacted with three different types of governmental authorities—the Jewish religious leaders (e.g., Pharisees, Sadducees, and the Sanhedrin), the quasi-Jewish Herodian kings, and the appointed Roman governors in their territory, such as Pontius Pilate. Jesus encountered Pilate immediately prior to His crucifixion in A.D. 30. During His final days, Jesus stood before all three forms of government during His pre-crucifixion trials. These were very difficult waters to navigate, since there were *three* major oppressive systems of authority-government operating in the first century in Judea and Samaria. Each tugged in different directions. Today we think it is difficult to deal with one governmental authority over us.

Jesus was also familiar with some of the regional military leaders assigned to secure taxation and maintain open trade routes. Jesus would have known some of the soldiers, termed "legionnaires" and their commanders, the "centurions." A centurion (or in Greek, kenturion) commanded approximately 80 legionnaires. Judea was not a popular assignment, and the monotheistic Jews had caused considerable discomfort for their Roman governors. The Romans were polytheistic and valued Greco-Roman philosophy, religion-mythology, and accumulation of mental knowledge in their worldview. The two religious and social cultures were clashing profoundly in Judea and Samaria. The Hebraic and Greco-Roman worldviews were entirely incompatible.

The legionnaires and centurions were disciplined and hardened military men. They formed the most effective military machine of any nation to that point in time. They were top of the line. A centurion was required to demonstrate fearlessness and stamina. They were known to march up to 20 miles per day while wearing or carrying up to 90 lbs. of weaponry and gear. They carried a double-edged sword (in Latin, gladius) for short-range combat, a dagger, several spears and thrusting javelins, various types of protective armor, and personal provisions. I personally have experienced a hint of what it might have been like to be armed as a centurion, as I occasionally speak and preach at conferences wearing a museum replica of first century centurion's armor. While wearing the steel armor, I often speak about Ephesians chapter 6.

So, what motivated the centurions stationed in Judea and Samaria? Why would they want to serve in that distant land? Perhaps career advancement or financial rewards. Some centurions were sufficiently successful in their careers that they might attain the status of an Equestrian. This was the equivalent of upper middle-class status in Western society today, albeit a difficult accomplishment *vis-à-vis* the ruling Patrician aristocratic landowners in Rome and its conquered territories.

Why Did God Use the *Written* Word?

Have you pondered why God placed His Word in written form as the most reliable source for spiritual food? How about the illiterate masses of the world? Are there not more than a billion people and many of the people groups of the world who can't read or who can't read the Bible in their own native tongue? If you can't read the Bible, how can you be saved by Yeshua and become His disciple? This situation should stimulate and encourage us to support organizations devoted to reaching the illiterate and underserved people groups of the world. I admire the Wycliffe Bible Translator missionaries who often work for decades in difficult circumstances to prepare portions of the Bible in local languages. My friends, Chuck and Barb Michaels, have spent much of their adult lives in Papua New Guinea for this cause. They even witnessed the martyrdom of a dear Christian colleague while there. Just think about the privileges we have in the Western World, not only with the written Bible, but access to so many Judeo-Christian resources that we take for granted.

Chapter 2

ENDNOTES

CAUTION REGARDING THE TERM "COVENANT"

Some believers speak positively about desiring to establish "covenant" relationships with churches, groups, and other people. In support they often mention the unique relationship established between David and Jonathan. The Holy Spirit has quickened my spirit to an alarm concerning the inappropriate and frequent of use of the term "covenant." The Scriptures are filled with examples admonishing us to not make oaths or covenants (see Mt. 5:33-37). Most of us have two primary covenants. The first is the relationship between believers and God, and the second is the relationship between husbands and wives. All other covenants should be avoided or entered into with great caution and only after serious evaluation. Covenants are serious "contracts" and they can't be broken or modified after the fact. They are binding. They must be fulfilled precisely as pledged (see Gal. 3:15). "*Above all, my brothers, do not swear—not by heaven or by earth or by anything else. Let your 'yes' be yes, and your 'no' be no, or you will be condemned*" (Jas. 5:12).

It is safe to speculate that many people engage others in binding covenants, because of the general lack of honesty, honor, and dependability in society today. Most people can't be relied upon to do what they say they will do. So, in order to make the stakes higher, someone requesting action by another person uses this term "covenant" to attempt to place an element of "bite behind the bark." Avoid it at all cost.

I strongly encourage you—simply speak the truth in love, and refuse to be encumbered by others, including well-intentioned believers and church leaders. Covenants with men and women should be unnecessary at least most of the time, and should be strongly avoided. For instance, God detests divorce (see Mal. 2:16), because a man and a woman are literally breaking their highest oath on Earth. But, our God is not a covenant breaker. His words have everlasting meaning and should be respected in obedience. Many have entered covenant relationships in ignorance, and some of these relationships are unholy and are used by the devil to grant him legal access and influence in our lives. We should seek to remedy this if at all possible, and to discourage oath making. Please preserve the term "covenant" for its right and exalted position of meaning.

RECOMMENDED BOOKS

- *Biography of Hudson Taylor* — by Vance Christie
- *Dwight L. Moody, The American Evangelist* — by Bonnie Harvey
- *William Carey, Father of Missions* — by Sam Wellman
- *George Mueller, Man of Faith* — by Bonnie Harvey
- *George Whitefield, Pioneering Evangelist* — by Bruce & Beck Durost Fish
- *Johnathan Edwards, The Great Awakener* — by Helen Hosier
- *Biography of Rees Howells—Intercessor* — by Norman Grubbs
- *Watchman Nee, Man of Suffering* — by Bob Laurent
- *The Heavenly Man* — by Brother Yun (with Paul Hattaway)
- *The Final Quest* — by Rick Joyner
- *The Flames of Rome, Pontius Pilate, and Josephus* — by Paul L. Maier
- *Faith — The Link With God's Power* — by Reinhard Bonnke
- *Experiencing God* — by Henry Blackaby
- *The Future War of the Church* — by Chuck D. Pierce & Rebecca Wagner Sytsema
- *Lord—I Want to Know You* — by Kay Arthur
- *The Coming Prophetic Revolution* — by Jim W. Goll
- *Intercession: The Power and Passion to Shape History* — by Jim W. Goll
- *Intercessory Prayer* — by Dutch Sheets
- *The Anointing: Yesterday, Today, Tomorrow* — by R.T. Kendall
- *In Pursuit of His Glory* — by R.T. Kendall
- *Surprised by the Power of the Spirit* — by Jack Deere
- *Thrones of Our Soul* — by Paul Keith Davis

CONTACT THE AUTHOR

info@pathclearer.com
and
www.pathclearer.com
www.tomdooley.org

PATH CLEARER, INC.
PO Box 661466
Birmingham, Alabama
35266-1466 USA

ABOUT THE AUTHOR

Dr. Thomas P. Dooley is the founder of Path Clearer Inc., with the goal to influence millions by communicating Judeo-Christian truth. Dr. Dooley is a prophetic preacher to the nations. Tom has a diverse professional background and is active in various ministries around the globe. He was a farm boy who subsequently became a scientist, professor, and entrepreneur. Tom has a Ph.D. in molecular biology and has worked in drug discovery research in various positions in the pharmaceutical industry and academia. He was one of the youngest recipients of a prestigious "endowed chair" (professor) position. He has published approximately 65 scientific articles, and has received research grants, patents for inventions, and many professional awards. Dr. Tom Dooley is a scientist-entrepreneur, who knows well the risk-reward relationship in the scientific and business worlds. He was the founder and CEO of two scientific companies within different industry sectors.

Dr. Tom Dooley has a diverse set of perspectives seldom provided by other authors on Judeo-Christian truth. He addresses these issues from solid biblical and firsthand perspectives as one accustomed to living in risk-taking belief in action. *Praying Faith* is presented in an exhorting direct style without sugarcoating the tough biblical concepts of genuine faith. A book written on the topic of faith by a successful scientist is a remarkable irony! It is the author's desire to see all *believers* become *disciples* within the Kingdom of God and demonstrating *risk-taking belief in action.*

Additional copies of this book and other
book titles from DESTINY IMAGE are
available at your local bookstore.

For a bookstore near you, call 1-800-722-6774.

Send a request for a catalog to:

Destiny Image® Publishers, Inc.

P.O. Box 310
Shippensburg, PA 17257-0310

*"Speaking to the Purposes of God for This
Generation and for the Generations to Come"*

**For a complete list of our titles,
visit us at www.destinyimage.com**